Managing Developmental Civil Society Organizations

Praise for this book

'Packed with hard-won insights based on the author's longstanding and unrivalled personal experience working in the civil society organization field, and drawn from his wide-ranging knowledge of relevant ideas, concepts and literature, this book is unlike any other you will read on the real worlds of civil society organizations. Read it – and be inspired!'

Professor David Lewis, Department of Social Policy,
London School of Economics & Political Science

'Unravelling civil society and then explaining how to make developmental organizations effective is a tricky challenge. It takes a person of Richard Holloway's insights and experience to do so in a real-life, practical way. Avoiding confusing theories and jargon, this book's comprehensive guidance draws on and revisits proven ideas and tools that can feed confidence about what to do and how in the messy work for sustainable change towards social justice. It is not just recommended reading to those new to the field. Old hands would do well to reflect on the text as they deal with disruptive forces that are the daily reality of management with pressures to "follow the (foreign) money", often at the cost of identity and values.'

Alan Fowler is an emeritus professor of the
International Institute of Social Studies in the Hague.

'Richard Holloway has distilled key lessons from decades of experience with strengthening civil society organizations around the world in this book. It offers practical advice for building civil society organizations to foster constructive social change in many different contexts.'

L. David Brown, Senior Research Fellow (retired),
Hauser Center for Nonprofit Organizations, Harvard University

'Congratulations! This is an invaluable book for those working in civil society organizations. It provides those whose hands are on the helms excellent guidelines on how to plan and execute their CSOs' work, mobilize the resources needed and dodge the dangers that confront them. It is written by one of today's most able development practitioners and the sheer immensity and diversity of his experience is evident in every page of this compelling book.'

John Clark, Chair of Board, Partnership for Transparency Fund

Managing Developmental Civil Society Organizations

Richard Holloway

PRACTICAL ACTION
Publishing

Practical Action Publishing Ltd
The Schumacher Centre,
Bourton on Dunsmore, Rugby,
Warwickshire, CV23 9QZ, UK
www.practicalactionpublishing.org

A catalogue record for this book is available from the British Library.
A catalogue record for this book has been requested from the Library of Congress.

ISBN 9781853399084 Hardback
ISBN 9781853399091 Paperback
ISBN 9781780449081 Library Ebook
ISBN 9781780449098 Ebook

Citation: Holloway, R., (2015) *Managing Developmental Civil Society Organizations*, Rugby, UK: Practical Action Publishing, <http://dx.doi.org/10.3362/9781780449081>.

Since 1974, Practical Action Publishing has published and disseminated books and information in support of international development work throughout the world. Practical Action Publishing is a trading name of Practical Action Publishing Ltd (Company Reg. No. 1159018), the wholly owned publishing company of Practical Action. Practical Action Publishing trades only in support of its parent charity objectives and any profits are covenanted back to Practical Action (Charity Reg. No. 247257, Group VAT Registration No. 880 9924 76).

The views and opinions in this publication are those of the author and do not represent those of Practical Action Publishing Ltd or its parent charity Practical Action. Reasonable efforts have been made to publish reliable data and information, but the authors and publisher cannot assume responsibility for the validity of all materials or for the consequences of their use.

Cover design by Mercer Design
Typeset by Allzone Digital Services Ltd
Printed in the UK

FSC

Contents

http://dx.doi.org/10.3362/9781780449081.000

Figures and boxes

Figures

Boxes

Preface

The context for this book is international development work and the place that citizens' institutions have in this area.

Anyone involved in development work will be aware of the huge numbers of civil society organizations (CSOs) that exist all over the world (the only exception is perhaps North Korea). They will also be aware of the confusion in many people's minds about what they are, how they work, to whom they are responsible, and what they have been able to achieve. This book is intended to clarify such issues, but is primarily intended to help those who have chosen to work in this field to understand better what they are doing, and what else they might do in the future.

There are many ways in which people are involved with CSOs:

- Citizens may be concerned with an issue or a cause that is important to them and that they want to do something about – and feel that they can do this best by joining others who feel the same way. Examples are a mother who has a disabled child, a student who seeks to combat corruption, a small trader who wants affordable credit, or a slum dweller who cannot get clean water.
- Citizens may be encouraged by people outside their community to join together in a group or association to deal with an issue. Examples are a group formed by a government body to build a dam, a group formed by an NGO to encourage primary healthcare, or a group encouraged by outsiders to join a national rally.
- Members of a CSO already working together on a topic that concerns them greatly may be trying to find the resources that will allow them to do more and be more effective.
- Members of an NGO (that is, a more formal CSO) may be looking for other CSOs to work with that they consider are likely to be committed, competent, and able to undertake development work of one kind or another.
- Government officials at the local or national level may find themselves approached by many different citizens' groups with many different agendas, but may not know how to deal with them.
- Professional funders of CSOs – either from bilateral or multilateral organizations, from international NGOs, or from international foundations – will be looking to support effective organizations that support the interests of the funders and that can be relied on to use their finances diligently, honestly, and capably.

There is an unfortunate tendency for this last group – professional funders of CSOs – to take on a role that is too dominant. Donor funding does not define

CSOs – they existed before foreign donors, and they can exist without foreign donors.

This book is to help those who are involved with CSOs to understand:

- what a CSO is and what civil society is as a whole;
- how they can best think through their contribution to development, and how to structure themselves to do this best;
- how they can best relate to the other important institutions in the world they inhabit – the people, the government, businesses, the media, and international agencies;
- how they can mobilize the resources they need to operate and be effective;
- how they can be sustainable over time.

It is also intended to help those involved with CSOs to deal with the fields in which there are the greatest gaps between rhetoric and reality: participation, integrity, constituencies, results, and independence. Finally, it discusses the greatest dangers that CSOs face in the future: donor dependence, irrelevance in wider strategic thinking, and inability to maintain a strong organization.

The book is based on a long career working in the civil society field in over 30 countries around the world, and has many references to where further information can be accessed. The author has had little experience in Latin America and so the book has few examples from the work of CSOs in that region.

I hope that those who use this book (not just *read* this book) will find it useful and that they can do better development work as a result. It is a practitioner's book, and does not attempt intellectual analysis of the concepts with which it deals. It will be successful if readers who are involved with CSOs are helped to be more effective in their involvement.

Origins of this book

This book derived from 'Establishing and Running an Advocacy NGO', produced for Pact Inc. The content has been completely revised for this book, but still refers to borrowed and acknowledged material from a variety of other sources that readers and practitioners are urged to access as well. Here is a selection:

Adirondack, Sandy, (1989) *Just About Managing: A Guide to Effective Management for Voluntary Organisations and Community Groups*, London: LVSC.

Camay, Phiroshaw, and Gordan, Anne, (1997) *Advocacy in Southern Africa: Lessons for the Future*, Johannesburg: CORE.

Easterly, William, (1995) *Checklist of NGO Organisational Development: Characteristics of NGOs at Different Stages*, Washington, DC: Pact.

Fowler, Alan, (1997) *Striking a Balance: A Guide to Enhancing the Effectiveness of Non-government Organisations in International Development*, London: Earthscan.

Holloway, Richard, (1996) *Capacity Building of Southern NGOs and CBOs*, Lusaka: Pact Zambia (internal unpublished document).

Holloway, Richard, (1997) *Objectives Oriented Project Planning*, Washington, DC: Pact.

Holloway, Richard, (2004) *NGO Corruption Fighter's Resource Book: How NGOs Can Use Monitoring and Advocacy to Fight Corruption*, New York: IMPACT.

Institute for Development Research., (1989) *Managing Organisational Change*, Boston, MA: Institute for Development Research.

Norton, Michael (ed.), (1997) *The World Wide Fundraisers Handbook: A Guide to Fundraising for Southern NGOs and Voluntary Organisations*, London: Directory for Social Change.

Organisational Capacity Assessment Tool (OCAT), (1995), Washington, DC: Pact.

CHAPTER 1

What is civil society and what are civil society organizations?

Civil society

A tremendous amount has been written on this subject, but, in essence, civil society is the associational life of the citizens of a country when they are not associating to govern a country (i.e. they are non-government) and not associating to make a personal profit (i.e. not for profit), but they *are* associating with some specific aim in view (i.e. not just for relaxation or recreation). It is based on the belief that non-political, non-profit-making citizens, when they are in association with others who share the same views, can be very effective and can effect change, and this change can be progressive.

When citizens band together to effect change for the better, they can be a tremendous force for good. A local association in India, MKSS (Mazdoor Kisan Shakti Sangathan), started work in 1994 by trying to identify where corrupt payments were being made in local food-for-work programmes in Rajasthan. Nine years later, and with the support of many organizations, they ended up getting parliament to pass the Freedom of Information Act 2005, which has dramatically changed the way in which the Indian government does business and protects the rights of citizens.

This chapter is about the kinds of association that have a developmental purpose: that is, those that try to improve, at different levels and in different ways, the situation of the poor and powerless in the countries in which they work.

The chapter starts by positing that there are three different sectors in any society: the government (the public sector), business (the private for-profit sector), and citizens (the private not-for-profit sector). Boundaries are intentionally fuzzy, and the relative sizes of the different sectors may vary between countries, but a basic typology for the three sectors of society is shown in Figure 1.1.

The three sectors

Government controls the structures of a country within its constitution. Its power is derived from the income that it receives from state assets, taxes, and international aid. It controls the means of violence in the country through the police and the armed forces.

http://dx.doi.org/10.3362/9781780449081.001

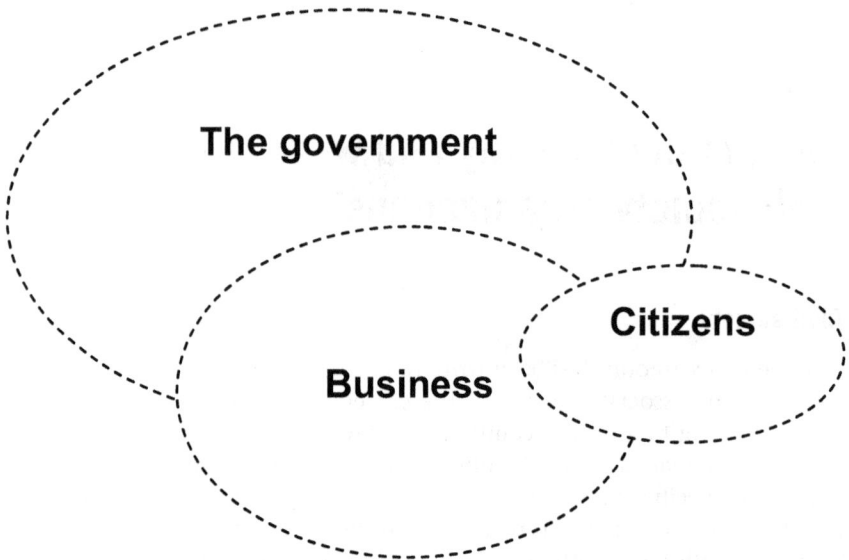

Figure 1.1 The three sectors of society

Business is responsible for the supply and transformation of goods and services in the country, acting within the law. Its power is derived from the income it receives from trading, natural resource exploitation, and service provision. In a capitalist system, it controls the provision of goods and services at prices that are acceptable to the public and favourable to businesses.

Civil society provides opportunities for citizens to associate together based on topics that they consider important and on which they want action. Its power derives from citizens' persuasion and joint action, and its income comes from voluntary donations of time and money, both from the affected citizens and from supporters of those citizens – both inside and outside the country.

Civil society in the development field is often the structure within which a citizen who has strong feelings about the need for change, particularly reform to improve the situation of the poor and powerless, chooses to operate. He or she feels that something can be done if they associate with other people to try to bring about change on many different levels, from the village to the nation.

Before we drill down into civil society and civil society organizations (CSOs), however, there are a number of points that need to be noted.

1. While we believe that it has a very important role in development, civil society supplements the work of the two other important players – government and business – and could not exist without them. The government of a country sets the scene and the context for what happens in that country (although there may, in some countries, be forces contesting to become the government), and the business sector pays taxes that allow the government to exist financially. Later in the book,

we will look at the contributions of government and business and how civil society can relate to them.

2. Citizens are essential to civil society, but also play roles within government and business. A citizen can be a government employee, his or her family may run a small clothing business, and, in addition, he or she may belong to a school alumni association, a faith or religious group, an ethnic association, and many more. If the citizen is very concerned about domestic violence, he or she might belong to a CSO that addresses this topic. If the citizen feels strongly about development issues, and if there is a cause that is dear to his or her heart, it is likely that he or she will choose CSOs as the channel for his or her aspirations and commitments. We should not forget, however, that the citizen will also exist in many other circles and contexts.

3. The sectoral boundaries within a society are fuzzy. Not only do citizens have many roles in all the sectors, but it can be difficult to understand in which sector some institutions fit. Is a political party part of government or civil society? Is a cooperative a business or does it fit within civil society? Is a not-for-profit business (or a social enterprise) a business or part of civil society? Learning more about CSOs helps us to answer these questions.

Civil society organizations

Any time that citizens associate together we can legitimately call the association that they have formed a CSO. This is the larger, all-inclusive word that contains within it a number of different types of organization: non-governmental organizations (NGOs), community-based organizations (CBOs), and faith-based organizations (FBOs).

Non-governmental organizations

From the start of the United Nations until the first Earth Summit in Rio de Janeiro in 1992, all non-government, non-profit developmental organizations were called NGOs. At the Earth Summit, the concept of a civil society, as opposed to a state-controlled society, became very common (Poland's Solidarinosc led the way as an independent trade union), making the terms 'civil society' and 'civil society organization' (CSO) more common and more widely used. Other people, particularly from the global South, pointed out that 'non-government' frequently translated into 'anti-government' in either the language or the attitudes of their countries. This was unhelpful – and indeed often harmful – to civil society, and was another reason why the positive 'civil society' was more attractive than the negative 'non-government'. In common usage in 2015, NGO is the term used to describe larger, formally registered CSOs that often derive their funding from foreign sources. NGO often subdivides into NNGOs (national NGOs) and INGOs (international NGOs).

Community-based organizations

These are associations of people who come from a common (and limited) geographical area and who have a common agenda for change. CBOs are based on membership. Usually, but not always, they rely on voluntary staff (as opposed to paid labour). It is quite possible for many CBOs to federate into organizations that go beyond limited community boundaries; this then becomes a federation of CBOs.

Faith-based organizations

These are organizations of people whose common denominator is belonging to a particular faith (usually Islam, Christianity, Buddhism, or Hinduism) and the way that this faith operates in the field of development. Depending on the country and its history, such faith-based organizations may be very large indeed and form a parallel educational or health structure to the government. In some cases, FBOs offer their services only to people who belong to the same faith; in others, the services they offer are available to all, without discrimination.

Non-state actors

There is one further category that readers may be familiar with: non-state actors. This term was coined by the Cotonou Agreement of 2000 and defines the kind of CSOs that the European Union is prepared to fund. In most cases, it is synonymous with civil society and includes non-profit associations of for-profit entities, such as chambers of commerce.

CHAPTER 2
Three kinds of civil society organization

Citizens join or support a great variety of organizations – everything from a local farmers' group or wives' club to a national organization like the Red Cross or Red Crescent Society. Many local and traditional organizations are well known only by the people of a particular area or language group, and are unknown outside that locality. Examples are the age sets of the Maasai people in Kenya, the *arisan* of Java, and the *stokvel* of South Africa.

In order for us to appreciate the richness of associational life, we need some tools with which we can 'unpack' such richness. We can usefully identify two broad categories of citizen organizations – mutual benefit organizations and public benefit organizations – but this should be followed by a warning note about a third category: 'pretenders'.[1] Each of these categories then has a variety of sub-categories. Figure 2.1 illustrates the different categories of citizen organizations found in the civil society of most countries. There may well be other categories; continual research is needed to understand the many, many ways in which citizens associate together for the purposes of change and progress. As an example, Cyclone Nargis in Myanmar in 2008 produced a flowering of citizen initiatives to help those affected by it – all the more noticeable because the Myanmar government at that time, and until recently, had not allowed formal non-government civil society organizations (CSOs).

When looking at these categories, however, we should not be tempted to think too formally about such organizations. Civil society also includes such ephemeral forms as demonstrations or boycotts where citizens come together for a particular purpose and disband after the purpose is achieved. These forms of loose collective behaviour by citizens are important, particularly when there are state prohibitions on more formal structures; in fact, many people would say that 'popular movements' are the purest form of CSO.

Two kinds of civil society organization and the pretenders

Let us look at these suggested two (plus one) major categories of citizen organizations. This book suggests that these categories fit the kinds of associational life that exists in the world today, and a review of them may help a CSO consider whether it could usefully modify or modulate into a different kind of organization.

Mutual benefit organizations

These comprise individuals who join together to form an organization in which they are members, in which they have a governance function to elect office

http://dx.doi.org/10.3362/9781780449081.002

```
                    ┌─────────────────────────┐
                    │    The nation state      │
                    └─────────────────────────┘
```

Public sector	Business sector	Civil society sector

The business sector	The media	Parliament and judiciary	The executive

Institutions of a civil society

Independent accountability institutions	Universities	Civil society organizations	Local authorities

Mutual benefit organizations (Benefiting their members)	Public benefit organizations (Benefiting the public)	Unacceptable organizations (Neither benefiting their members nor the public)

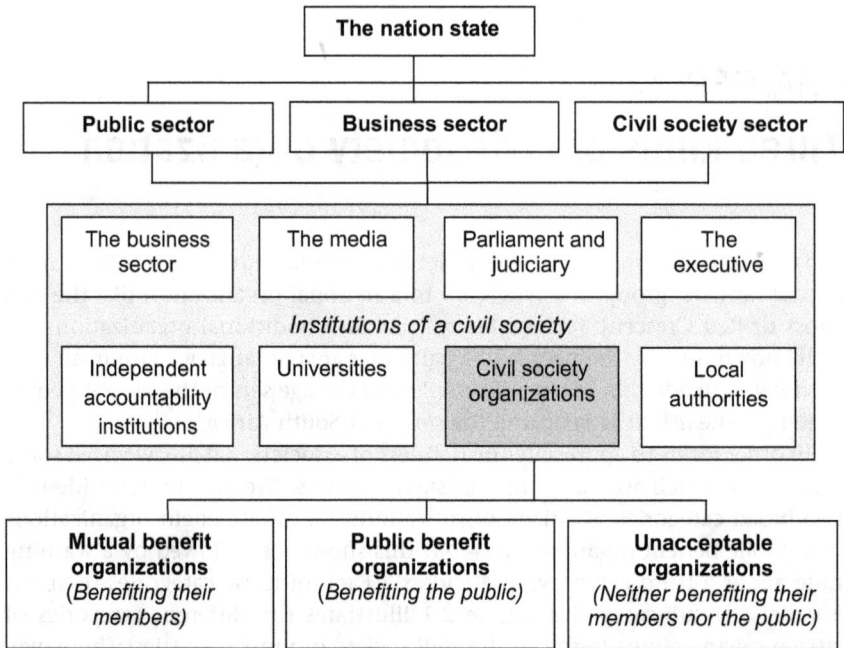

- Religious groups
- Indigenous community organizations and federations
- Induced community organizations and federations
- Ethnic organizations
- Political parties (?)
- Employment-related associations
  - Professional
  - Trade unions
  - Chambers of commerce
  - Trade associations
- Cooperatives (?)
- People's organizations or social movements
- Recreational or cultural organizations

- Private philanthropic
- Public philanthropic
- Religious
- Civic organizations
  - Law
  - Governance
  - Democracy
- NGOs (developmental and charitable)
  - Imlementation
  - Networking
  - Research
  - Advocacy
  - Apex (coordinating NGOs)
  - Umbrella (fund channelling)
- Non-profit companies

- Organizations promoting violence and extremism
- Organizations pretending to be CSOs but only seeking tax benefits for themselves or their business
- Organizations claiming to represent a constituency but really controlled by a politician, business, or government
- Organizations collecting funds that do not intend to give them to the needy

Figure 2.1 An overview of the state, civil society institutions and civil society organizations

bearers, and from which, as members, they derive benefits. Such organizations may be very small – community organizations in a particular geographical area – or large and national in scope. Typical examples are cooperatives, trade unions, professional associations, and village self-help groups. They may also contain an ephemeral category, as mentioned earlier, for such things as boycotts or strikes.

Public benefit organizations

These are groups where those responsible for founding the organization aim to benefit citizens whom they have identified as needing help. The people who govern or are members of the organization are not themselves the targets or beneficiaries of the organization, and those governing the organization are appointed at the initiative of committed individuals (often in the form of a board) and are not drawn from those identified as needing help.

These organizations can also range from very small to very large. Their mandate comes from the common perceptions and values of self-selected citizens. And while they are invariably public-spirited in nature, board members are more often than not accountable to their organization's governance structure and to the law under which they are incorporated, not to those who benefit from their services. Those whose interests are served, therefore, do not set the mandate of the organization, as they do in mutual benefit organizations.

Typical examples of public benefit organizations are foundations, NGOs, and charitable organizations.

Pretenders

Because so much attention (and so much money) has been paid to CSOs, spurious groups of people have appeared that pretend to be CSOs but actually belong to the state or the business sector, or are purely self-interested. These represent neither membership organizations nor organizations of committed individuals who wish to benefit others; instead, they comprise individuals who are trying to earn money or power for themselves, their political party, or their business.

These three broad categories have sub-categories within them. When we look at these, we see the accuracy of Alan Fowler's statement about civil society:

> Too seldom is the point made that civil society is a messy arena of competing claims and interests between groups that do not necessarily like each other, as well as a place for mediation and collaboration (Fowler, 2001).

Note that so far this chapter has not discussed donor funding. To pick up a point made earlier, an understanding of the nature and value of civil society is not defined by the donors or by the approach a donor may have to them.

Mutual benefit organizations

The following is an overview of the kinds of organization typically found in this category, though – there may well be other local variations, as suggested earlier:

- faith-based organizations;
- indigenous CBOs;
- introduced (or induced) CBOs;
- ethnic or traditional organizations;
- political parties (?);
- employment-related organizations (trade unions, professional associations, trade associations);
- cooperatives (?);
- people's organizations or social movements;
- student organizations;
- recreational or cultural organizations.

Faith-based organizations

These are associations that benefit the members of a particular faith-based grouping, either a common religion (such as Islam) or, more commonly, a particular sect or congregation within a specific religion.

Where faith-based groups offer benefits to the general public (schools or hospitals, for instance), they are listed under 'public benefit organizations'. This category is for a group defined by its faith, and identified more precisely by a particular sub-group within that faith, and that offers benefits to the members of that group. Such a group may be of great service to its members, helping them both spiritually and socially.

One of the worrying elements of contemporary civil society is that such groups have also shown themselves to be potential lightning rods for extremism, intolerance, and violence towards others. Charismatic people who have great potential for encouraging mutual tolerance between different faiths may lead such organizations. However, it is also possible that such organizations can be led autocratically, particularly if the leader claims divine guidance. Examples of mutual benefit, faith-based groups exist all over the world. In places where different faiths used to coexist, such groups have often polarized along religious or sect lines, turning to feuding and violence. In places where traditional life is a strong basis for religion, those traditions can define the mutual benefit organization.

Traditional organizations have a huge potential for community participation and governance according to accepted traditions. Yet, we should be aware that 'traditional' does not always mean 'beneficent'. Traditional CSOs are prone to being male-dominated, feudalistic autocracies that keep women and youth out of leadership positions.

Indigenous community-based organizations

These are indigenous organizations that reflect the interests and the culture of those who belong to a specific geographical community or who are the original inhabitants of a particular area. They may exist only at the time of a particular activity, such as joint work parties that are organized at village level to cultivate land for a common purpose, or to deal with a common problem (like a broken bridge or a land claim). They may also, however, be permanent, with a very strong political or cultural identity. In theory, traditional or customary organizations are immensely valuable for development and democratic governance, since they are (usually) well established within a community, command people's involvement, and are managed through local resources.

On the other hand, they may also involve unhelpful activities that are, for instance, harmful to women (associations to carry out female genital mutilation, for example) or to minority groups (such as homosexuals). They may be additionally harmful because they perpetuate autocratic governance that suppresses freedom of expression.

Introduced (or induced) community organizations

An introduced (or induced) community organization has been introduced from outside the area of operation, has been set up at the instigation of outsiders, and is endorsed or participated in (to varying degrees) by locals. It refers to community organizations that have been induced or introduced by the state, donors, NGOs, or other participants in the past, often defined by a specific government programme or project.

The intention of most introduced community organizations is that in time they will be accepted, absorbed, and 'mainstreamed' into people's lives so that they become thought of as 'indigenous' rather than imposed by outsiders. However, this rarely happens. A recurring difficulty in both the North and South is that the benefits (and thus the beneficiaries) of 'introduced' initiatives depend on outside resources (either government or non-government), with the organizational structure often lasting only as long as the resources keep flowing. Indeed, where outside resources are part of the induced CBO, its introduction may also create internal strife in the community as people fight over access to the outside funds.

Ethnic organizations

Ethnic organizations provide a sense of identity for many minority people, particularly against the dominating influence of the majority ethnicity. People coming from the same language group and often the same geographical background define these organizations. Language and geography still remain mobilizing forces even when the links people have to their ethnic origins are tenuous.

Ethnic groupings in major cities have had the useful function of helping their ethnic brothers and sisters acclimatize to city life. These organizations for mutual support and identity preservation help members of ethnic groups who are far from home. Unfortunately, another frequent aspect of ethnic associations is ethnic-based criminal gangs that can, for instance, control gambling, prostitution, protection, and drugs in many big cities.

In some countries, ethnic affiliations that were suppressed by a previous ruling autocracy for ideological and security reasons mushroom with liberalization of the regime and often become a driving force for ethnic cleansing initiatives.

Political parties

Some would say that political parties belong in the government sector rather than the citizen sector since, in effect, they are 'would-be governments'. For this reason, 'political parties' are listed above and in Figure 2.1 with a question mark. Before they succeed (or fail) in being elected to government, however, political parties have the potential to be powerful associational magnets for citizens with common interests or sets of values. In many western European countries during the 1920s, for example, 'political parties on the ground' were important catalysts for the growth of many kinds of CSOs. They also prepared the way for totalitarian governments, as in Germany and Italy.

Employment-related associations

This sub-category comprises organizations that represent people by virtue of their employment. This includes:

- trade unions that represent workers;
- modern sector employers' associations;
- professional associations of dentists, engineers, physicians, teachers, and so on;
- less formal associations of the self-employed, such as fishermen, weavers or potters.

Cooperatives

Just as political parties may be better represented by the government sector, so cooperatives may fit better within the business sector (which is why they also have a question mark after them in the list above and Figure 2.1), as they are associations of people who join together to engage in different kinds of business activity collectively. They have huge development potential, but in many countries they have been taken over by government departments and this has often stultified their growth, if not killed them altogether.

People's organizations or social movements

This covers a wide range of membership associations, which in turn represent a much larger group than a 'geographically bound' community. The term can also cover the non-military part of separatist organizations that are seeking to break away from a nation, or to preserve a political distinction. Some examples are:

- federations of large numbers of CBOs that have joined together at a sub-regional, regional, or national level;
- organizations representing broad categories of people, such as women, youth, or the disabled;
- issue-based membership organizations that, for example, oppose child labour or corruption or promote the causes of women. Such organizational bodies are also set up, for example, to get support for people whose livelihoods may be destroyed by large dam projects or environmentally destructive factories. Essentially temporal in nature, these organizations may cease to exist when the issue is resolved;
- mass-based membership organizations with a foundation in religion or politics. Their links to the grassroots offer particular advantages when they become involved in political advocacy work, but can be a source of fundamentalist ideas, too.

Large membership-based organizations have huge development and democratic potential when their membership is from the group that is suffering and needs help, either in the form of mobilizing resources or in their insistence on policy changes and implementation. One of the problems of these organizations is that they are very attractive to political parties for short-term gains, and are thus susceptible to political co-option.

Student organizations

In most countries, there are plenty of students and ex-students who form associations out of a variety of interests (to keep in touch with their alma mater and with their former peers, to shape the public life at their school or university, or to advocate for broader social, cultural, and political causes). In many countries, student organizations have played and continue to play a significant role in demonstrating against perceived and unresolved social injustice. Student organizations are also very attractive to politicians (as well as to extremists of all persuasions) who want to use students as 'shock troops' on behalf of one cause or another.

Recreational or cultural organizations

Such groups (sports clubs, bird-watching societies, choirs, and so on) have development potential because they bring people together in non-threatening ways for mutual interaction. This may be a very useful function if the society is polarized ethnically or tribally.

They also have strong possibilities in the field of social mobilization (men and women in sport who speak out against drug abuse, for instance), but for the most part they are not involved in development activities.

Public benefit organizations

Next is an overview of the kinds of organization typically found within the category of public benefit organizations. There may well be other local variations, as has been suggested previously.

Here we are dealing with organizations of people who wish to help other people. In some cases, they use their own resources to help; in others, they seek financing from a third group and act as intermediaries to make sure that donated money is used effectively and responsibly:

- private philanthropic bodies;
- public philanthropic bodies;
- faith-based organizations;
- location-based organizations;
- civic organizations;
- NGOs (of many types, as will be discussed later).

Private philanthropic organizations

These are organizations set up by wealthier members of a community that earmark money and resources for particular groups of people, with the organization's mandate often dictated by its founders or benefactors. Often such organizations have a strong charitable perspective: that is, they accept the status quo, do not try to change it, and see their role simply as helping the less fortunate. This contrasts with a developmental perspective in which the status quo is questioned and it is recognized that people need to help themselves. There also may be a public relations component for the benefactor and his or her family.

Public philanthropic organizations

These organizations, which usually take the form of a foundation, have been set up for the general public good by an individual, group of individuals, business, or government. Sometimes they act as a direct implementing or grant-giving foundation to benefit those who come within the terms of the foundation's charter. They may also be organizations such as Rotary clubs, Lions clubs, or service clubs of the business community that want to assist in development for an identified group. Other examples include the Ford Foundation and many community foundations. The existence of such organizations in the South is particularly important because they put decision-making about what should be supported into the hands of people in the country concerned instead of external donors from other countries.

Faith-based organizations

These are organizations that are based on religious principles or specific religious organizations, but do not limit their generosity and assistance to those who are from that particular religious group (unlike the membership-based religious organizations mentioned previously in the mutual benefit category). A person of any faith (or, indeed, no faith) is allowed to receive the benefits of the organization.

Many religious organizations have formed schools, universities, hospitals, and clinics that are open to all. Part of the subtext is sometimes the desired conversion of those benefiting from the services to the religion (or particular beliefs) of the service provider, but this is seldom a condition of attendance.

Location-specific philanthropic organizations

People who come from a particular area but are no longer living there form such organizations. They may be living in the capital city or even overseas.

Such organizations are increasing with migration to the cities and the break between people and their roots. They often set up local interest groups or councils that carry out the aims of the 'voluntarily displaced' people. People often come together for marriages or funerals, to meet with others who have come from the same place, and to discuss what they can do to help their 'home town'.

Civic organizations for political advocacy

Here we are referring to organizations that restrict their role to advocating for a change in laws, policies, regulations, or behaviour. They exist primarily at the international level and include groups such as Amnesty International, Greenpeace and Focus on the Global South.

However, as many autocracies move towards more liberal systems, these organizations are establishing themselves in individual countries. Still, they are less involved in playing an implementing role in projects or grassroots welfare and development activities than in general advocacy in support of overarching social and political reforms.

The increasing number of advocacy organizations that has begun to flourish throughout the world reflects two things: first, the energy of citizens promoting and embracing democracy and democratic reforms; and second, the large amount of funds that have been provided to organizations (particularly in the South) willing to get involved in such work.

This proliferation of funding results from the desire of many international donors to help countries of the South better understand and adopt democratic ideals and practices, with citizens' organizations being the key to spreading the word. One of the main unanswered questions with regard to civic organizations (as with development and welfare NGOs) is who they represent and what their actual constituencies are. A number of civic organizations represent little more than the small number of people who make up their staff. While they are legitimately entitled to express their point of view, their claims to represent a larger constituency sometimes need to be checked. When such organizations claim to be acting for the good of the nation, for example, it is important to ascertain just how deep are their organizational roots – in the nation's villages or urban slums, for instance.

Development and welfare NGOs

These are organizations started by citizens with the intention of improving the situation of those who are disadvantaged or a situation that affects the whole country. They do this through a variety of roles, none of which are exclusive:

- implementing;
- advocacy;
- networking;
- research and think tanks;
- capacity building and support;
- representation.

They are usually legally registered under the laws of a country, have a formal governance structure, and are equipped with paid staff (although this is not as likely with smaller NGOs). In the global South, the fields in which they work are usually health, education, agriculture, self-employment, family planning and family welfare, community development, environment, gender, good governance, and anti-corruption issues.

NGOs are often intermediary organizations that collect resources from one group of people in order to provide services to another group who are targeted because of their poverty, powerlessness, or need for services. They may have a membership structure for governance purposes, but they are not mutual benefit organizations.

The best local and international NGOs see how important it is that the problems of the poor and disadvantaged with whom they work are understood by society at large, either regionally or nationally. Public education and social mobilization to sustain citizens' interest in the alleviation or eradication of the root causes of a region's or country's problems are thus of paramount concern to these NGOs.

The best also systematically build CBOs and people's organizations that will continue autonomously without the support of the local or international NGO. Many Northern NGOs working in international development, however, have cultivated a patron–client relationship with the organizations they support. In many cases, the clients are interested in the patrons only for as long as a stream of development benefits continues to flow from the North.

In the best cases, NGOs (both national and foreign) carry out exercises that identify needs and include participation in the design and implementation of programmes to respond to those needs. When they operate in such a fashion, it is clear that they have a constituency that is supporting their work (and a mandate from the people they want to help). Unfortunately, there is little to force an NGO to work in this way, and an increasing number of NGOs decide which programmes they want to undertake without any input from their constituency.

Implementation

Here, an NGO's main work is carrying out grassroots activities to improve the lives of the target group. They are usually organized on a project basis, which means a time-specific period with a pre-agreed budget. This is usually to fit in with the administrative convenience of a donor (from the global North or South) that gives grants only on a project basis. As many NGOs know, real life does not follow a project format, and projects force NGOs into an unrealistic method of working with their target group.

Advocacy

We have dealt with organizations that push for political and social reform in the previous section. This section relates to organizations that pursue advocacy strategies to support the particular fields in which they work – farmers' rights, children's rights, rights of the disabled, and so on. Here, the NGO's work involves not only carrying out grassroots activities, but also trying to change public policy. They are best placed to do this because of their experience in the field. They know what works and what does not, and, perhaps most importantly, what the absence of (or the wrong application of) a government policy means in practice.

Networking

Here, the main activity of the NGO is coordinating other NGOs that work in a particular geographical area or field of work. Networking is particularly relevant to advocacy work, from ad hoc participation to formal alliances, because it enables a larger aggregation of organizations to put themselves forward as agents of change.

Research and think tanks

The main activity here is researching and analysing particular issues. NGOs are rarely large enough to have their own research and analysis unit, but they often make alliances, for example with university departments that carry out such work. It is more common for a number of university researchers to form an off-campus organization that operates as a think tank and is registered as an NGO. Such organizations offer their services to NGOs, to business, and to local or national government.

Capacity building and support

A number of NGOs have realized that smaller CSOs have a great need to build their institutional, organizational, and technical capacities. To this end, they have set themselves up as specialist support NGOs to help less developed CSOs. In an increasing number of cases, these organizations become contractors to donors, who use the term 'capacity building' to mean the ability to manage the bureaucracy required in receiving grants in the form demanded by the donor.

Representation

Here, the purpose is to provide a form of liaison between NGOs and government. A truly representative organization will have some democratic structure that allows for: 1) membership; and 2) elections to select those who will represent the NGO (sub-)sector to the government, or to donors. Examples might be NGOs in the education or primary healthcare field.

Many assume that NGOs are closer to the people's real needs because they are NGOs and not government. This may well be true in many cases, but it should nonetheless be verified on a case-by-case basis. Some NGOs have been set up as a means of self-employment and do not work together with those they target. It is also thought that some NGOs are established solely as a means of accessing government funds. This point is discussed in the following section.

Pretenders (or private benefit organizations)

This section covers a variety of organizations that misrepresent themselves by pretending to be independent, public benefit citizens' organizations, when really they are something altogether different. The reason why it is important to shed light on this group is that in many countries the public is fast becoming cynical about the civil society sector and its claims. The proliferation of 'pretender organizations' is a major reason for this. These organizations might have begun life as genuine public benefit organizations, but they have evolved into employment- and income-creating vehicles for their founders.

- *GONGOs*. These claim to be NGOs but are, in fact, government-organized NGOs (GONGOs).
- *BONGOs*. This refers to business-owned NGOs. As with GONGOs, there is a real danger that 'pretenders' can muddy the waters for those businesses that have a genuine public-spirited desire to contribute to development and democratic governance and would like to use corporate social responsibility methods. BONGOs, however, are interested in getting NGO status so that, for instance, they can avoid taxes.

- *DONGOs.* Here we mean donor-owned NGOs, whereby donors set up 'shell NGOs' in order to carry out their own programmes without the complexity of having to identify and negotiate with indigenous NGOs. It is relatively simple for a donor to find a malleable and compliant 'NGO for hire' that will do whatever the donor contracts the NGO to do. The reason for having public benefit citizens' organizations is that citizens will, on their own, decide what they think needs doing to improve a particular situation. When a foreign donor in effect buys an NGO to do the donor's bidding, the integrity of citizens' organizations is called into question.

Putting it all together

As can be seen from the diverse list of functions and activities, CSOs can encompass everything from a chess club to a political advocacy organization, or a wheelchair users' group to a fundamentalist organization in support of ethnic cleansing. CIVICUS[2] uses the following definition:

> The sphere of institutions, organizations and individuals located between the family, the state and the market, in which people associate voluntarily to advance common interests (Holloway, 2001).

These common interests may be valuable in building a harmonious and egalitarian society, or they may be much more selfish and exclusive. When we look at the health of civil society and the effect of CSOs on a nation's health, we have to be very objective in looking at what CSOs actually do and what effects they have.

There is one last category of which we need to be aware. It does not come within our categories of CSOs since it is operating for profit, but it often carries out similar activities to CSOs. This is the development contractor – a for-profit business that often takes on development or social and humanitarian work. The government, a donor, or a foundation might pay it and it can operate on terms that do not maximize profit. At the end of the day, however, the contractor has to cover its costs and make a profit, and this will determine what it is able to do and at what cost.

Notes

1. The category of pretenders was first developed by Alan Fowler in his book *Striking a Balance* (2001).
2. CIVICUS is a global association of CSOs (<http://civicus.org>).

Reference

Fowler, A. (2001) *Striking a Balance: A Guide to Enhancing the Effectiveness of Non-government Organisations in International Development*, London: Earthscan.
Holloway, R. (2001) *Assessing the Health of Civil Society - a handbook for using the CIVICUS Index on Civil Society as a self-assessment tool*, CIVICUS.

CHAPTER 3

What is the best path to take for social change?

There is often a gap between those who espouse a 'good cause' and those who seriously want to be effective in doing something about it. Many people feel strongly about an issue but do not necessarily either start or join an organization dedicated to doing something about that issue. They may, for instance, not feel sufficiently motivated to do so, they may consider that as individuals they do not have enough to offer, or they may consider that they would like to address this issue through other means (for example, political agitation or articles in newspapers). For some, however, their interest in an issue or cause leads them to think that they should try to form an organization as the vehicle through which they will effect change. They feel that bringing together people who share the same values and similar motivations is the best way to bring about a change for the better.

What avenues are available to them? A new enthusiast for changing the world (or at least that part of the world most important to him or her) has basically three options:

1. *Government action*. He or she may decide that the way to go is to persuade the government of the need to support their ideas, so that the government will use the resources of the state and effect a change in national or local policy and practice. Since, in most democratic systems, the executive arm of government requires political direction, this may mean addressing politicians and political parties and persuading them to adopt new policies and to instruct government officials to implement them. The person taking this route understands that the resources available to government are control and enforcement (with sanctions and punishment for non-compliance with government orders) as well as encouragement and support, and that these can come from the use of government media and government funding.

2. *Commercial action*. He or she may feel that business – that is, the manufacturing, buying, and selling of products and services – is a more practical and workable way of effecting change. He or she will either seek to persuade existing businesses to help effect change or perhaps start a business with this aim. The resources available to business are persuasion of people to adopt and use affordable products and services that have some developmental impact. Such adoption and use has to result in profits for the business involved, since no business can continue to

http://dx.doi.org/10.3362/9781780449081.003

provide products and services, however worthy, without covering its costs and making a surplus to keep it in business.
3. *Citizen action.* He or she may feel that the option of working outside government and outside business, and relying on the enthusiasm and commitment of people to contribute their time, energy, and resources is the way to go. These resources are supplemented with funds that citizens agree to contribute or can persuade others to contribute.

What are the options?

This book is in favour of – and supports the option of – citizen action. But all new enthusiasts and agents of change need to consider the other options, balancing their good and bad points, and thinking about the possibilities of using elements from all three options. Let us, therefore, take an example of change that many would consider self-evident and work it through the different options. Let us take the example of sanitation – that is, the control of human waste so that it does not become a health hazard and bring disease to communities.

The government can design programmes to persuade people not to urinate or defecate in the open, to dispose of their waste in a hygienic manner, and to continue to do this. It can offer the carrot of full or partial help with building latrines, and the stick of punishing communities that do not implement the new programmes. Its effectiveness depends on the availability of government budgets, government officials to encourage, administer, and implement the programme, and the structure of government to execute such a programme.

The business world can sell products and services connected to sanitation that will be attractive to communities and persuade them to use them. These could be at a range of technologies and qualities, from concrete rings to help with dug latrines, through to flush toilets, soap, and disinfectants. Its effectiveness depends on the target population wanting to use the products and services it offers (although wants can be created through persuasion) and being able to buy them at a price that allows the business to make a profit, and thus stay in business supplying these products and services.

The citizens' world can persuade citizens to improve their lives by mutually deciding to change their behaviour, by providing them with knowledge of and access to new technologies, and by helping them to be mutually supportive in their joint commitment to sanitation. This depends on an accurate understanding of the citizens' appreciation of the problems, their determination to do something about them, their disposable income and spare time, and an ability to mobilize change agents to work with the target group, to mobilize people to work together and support each other, and to mobilize the resources to fund their programmes.

Likely problems with each option

It does not require a great deal of experience to identify the likely problems, in the real world, of each of these approaches.

The government option may well become a top-down programme enforced by officials who do not relate to the citizens' issues and who are under political pressure to make it work in order to please political leaders. It may be susceptible to corruption in the choice of suppliers of services and products, the prices paid, and the target families assisted. It may last for a limited period of time, and may not be something that the community is doing – or is prepared to continue to do – on its own because of its reliance on government handouts.

The business option may well never get started because there is not enough income to be made from selling sanitation services and products to poor people. It may be that it is difficult to design a business model that is a combination of selling profitable products and services and encouraging self-help, and difficult either to set up a decentralized manufacturing system or to distribute centrally produced products and services to remote communities.

The citizen action option may well misjudge people's concern to improve their own sanitation, misjudge community dynamics and leadership, find it difficult to identify locally acceptable change agents, and find it hard to design programmes with a balance between outside assistance and local self-help. Finally, it may be difficult to source funding, or funds may be available only for an arbitrary period of time that does not fit the time it takes to develop the ability of local citizens to take over a sustainable process.

The new enthusiast needs to decide which option he or she is going to choose, or what combination of options. There are many strong arguments for a combined approach that brings in the best approaches of government, business, and the citizen sector.

First, the enthusiast should conduct an objective assessment of the strong and weak points of the three options, together with a subjective assessment of which option he or she considers they are best suited to work with. If, on the basis of this, he or she decides to opt for the citizen action option, then they have to consider the organizational form most suited to their approach. What kind of citizens' organizations with what competences, what capacities, and what values best represents their desire to effect sustainable change? Which are likely to create awareness of a problem, motivate people, lobby for change, and promote new ways of thinking and acting?

The capacities and values needed for a citizens' organization

If the citizens' organization, or civil society organization (CSO), you want to create will continue to exist and be effective in the long term in the development of your country – and not collapse because it cannot attract the resources you require – then Figure 3.1 may be useful. It shows the capacities you need in their order of importance (top to bottom) and suggests the priorities and sequencing

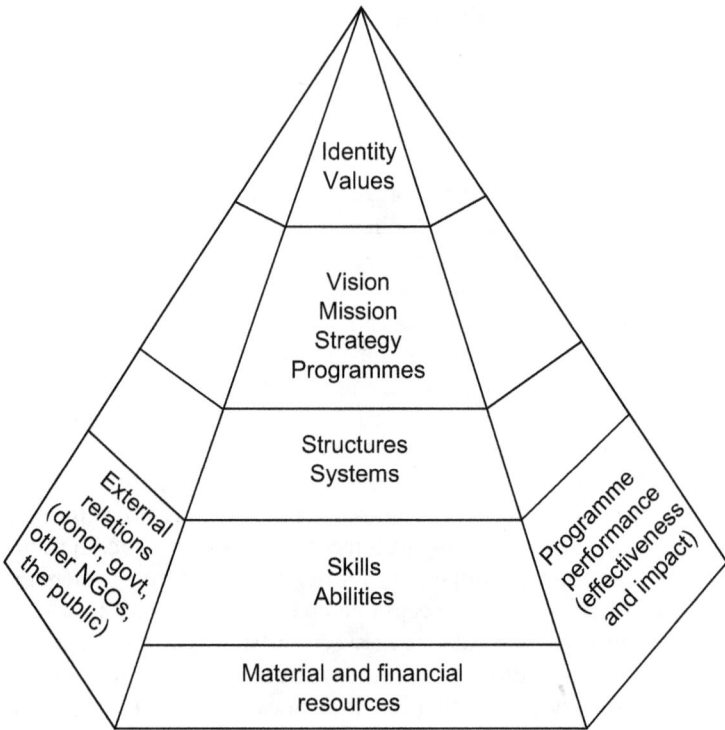

Figure 3.1 Hierarchical pyramid of capacities

for when you need to build capacity. Capacities in the upper levels need to be in place in order for capacities in the lower levels to be effective, therefore you need to build the upper ones first. Please look at the different levels of capacity. It is no use working to provide capacities in the lower levels of the pyramid until the capacities higher up the pyramid are functioning well.

Let us look at these different levels, starting from the top. Your CSO will need:

Identity and values

This means that a CSO knows what kind of organization it is, why it exists, and who it serves, and it operates with clear and openly expressed values. It understands that it is not a government department, nor is it a for-profit entity, but a non-government, not-for-profit entity with all that that entails.

Vision, mission, strategy and programmes

This means that a CSO has worked out what it wants to achieve in the long term, what it wants to achieve in the shorter term, why it wants to achieve this, what are the results it wants to get, and what general impact it wants to have.

Structures and systems

This means that a CSO understands how an organization works and what it requires to function well. We are talking about a professional, competent organization, not just a set-up that reflects a particular leader's personality.

Skills and abilities

This means that the CSO staff have the knowledge and training to do the things that the organization needs to do, in terms of both the programme and administration, and have demonstrated those skills and abilities.

Material and financial resources

This means that the CSO has the resources it needs to carry out its work, has been able to collect and manage such resources, knows how to use them, and knows how to demonstrate such use to others.

Look again at the pyramid to consider the hierarchy of levels and capacities. It is worth considering which capacity is dependent on which other capacity. Very many people who work with CSOs do not do this, and think that all capacities can be built at the same time. Please follow the relevant section on the diagram, starting at the bottom:

- It is no use providing an NGO with *material and financial resources* before the NGO has the skills and abilities to use those resources – they will be wasted or lost.
- It is no use building the NGO's *skills and abilities* if the NGO does not have the structures and systems to make use of those new skills and abilities – the skills and abilities will not be used and will be lost.
- It is no use having *systems and structures* in place unless the NGO is clear about its vision, mission, strategy and programmes. This can result in a CSO that is very efficient administratively but which does not achieve much.
- It is no use having a *vision, mission, strategy and programmes* in place if there are problems with the NGO's identity and values. The CSO needs to know who it is planning to help and why.
- *Identity and values* are the most important feature of any CSO. Is it really a serious, committed, non-government, not-for-profit entity? This needs to be checked.

Identity and values

Identity

Identity concerns what you are as an organization and where you are coming from in your desire to effect change. There is a very relevant legal phrase – *locus standi* – which means the basis for your actions. This reflects, for instance:

- whether you are a membership organization based on people who are affected by the issue of concern to the organization;
- whether you are an organization formed by people with a particular religious or ideological stance;
- whether you are an organization formed by people who have a strong identification with the problems of others, and want to do something about it;
- whether you are clear that you are trying to effect change through commitment to action that is not derived from seeking a profit, or derived from political power over other people.

Values

There are the usual values that CSOs hope to demonstrate, but consider whether there are others that you would like to add:

- *Participation.* This means that all those who are affected by the programmes of an organization should have some voice in deciding those programmes. CSOs should not implement programmes where the intended beneficiaries have not been consulted.
- *Transparency.* Because CSOs are voluntary organizations working in the public arena, and because they are often taking public funds, information on the work of the CSO should be publicly available and not hidden. CSOs should publicly announce what it is they want to do and publicly report on what it is they have achieved and with what resources.
- *Good governance.* CSOs should have a structure to govern their organization that is not made up of simply the director and the staff because of possible conflicts of interest. There should be a board of advisers.
- *Accountability.* CSOs usually accept money from people or organizations to carry out their work. They should be ready and able to explain what it is they are doing and the costs of doing it to the public, the government, the donors, the staff, and the board of advisers. They are set up to achieve desired results for their stakeholders, and they need to report back to their stakeholders on whether they succeeded in this or not.
- *Integrity.* CSOs should be honest in their dealings with the public and the people they want to help, always telling the truth. Leaders have a clear idea what is their own property and what belongs to the organization.
- *Commitment.* Once CSOs have decided on a problem that they want to overcome, and a programme by which they hope to do this, they should be determined to carry out this work as well as they can. They should be driven by the mission of their organization and not by the money that they may make.

CSOs define themselves by their values. Their values make them different from government and businesses. They are organizations of citizens who care about poverty, powerlessness, injustice, abuses of citizens' rights, and other important matters. They have put themselves forward to do something about this, and they have requested help from others to enable them to do this.

It is very important that your organization has integrity in the values that it espouses. If, for instance, you state that your organization is based on participation, but a short examination shows that your organization is a self-selected group of like-minded people who direct development projects for other people who are seen as only targets or beneficiaries, then it is likely that your credibility in this respect will be very fragile; likewise if you espouse gender equity but an examination reveals that all your board members and senior staff are men. And if you espouse transparency for your organization but do not make your financial accounts public, you are similarly open to the charge of hypocrisy.

CHAPTER 4

What is your civil society organization going to do?

The essence of a civil society organization

These days, the words 'civil society organization' (CSO) and 'doing development' very frequently include the assumption that the work will necessarily involve foreign donor funding. This introduces all sorts of issues that are not intrinsic to the idea of a group of citizens of a country getting together to promote change – particularly to reduce poverty. Those working with CSOs have become conditioned (almost addicted) to the idea that citizens who want to work outside government and outside for-profit businesses to reduce poverty will have to identify foreign donors; learn their language, systems, and procedures; 'sell' their proposals; and report on their progress in ways defined by such donors.

This confuses the essence of why people form a developmental CSO – what they aim to do with such an organization and what they hope to achieve. If we are not careful, developmental CSOs will become contractors to donors, with their vision, mission, strategy, and activities dictated by the source of the funding, rather than by the interest, commitment, and passion of citizens who care about change and reducing poverty.

The essence of a CSO is the commitment of citizens' time, energy, and common enthusiasm to something they believe in and want to achieve – not by instruction or compulsion, as governments do, nor by seeking profits, as businesses do, but by the aggregation of joint energy of people who believe in a cause, a problem to be solved, and a future different from the present. If that aggregation of joint energy without political or economic power is not there, then your organization is probably better off working through government or business.

Of course, funds are necessary to manage organizations and run programmes, but the funds should support the citizens' commitment to the cause, and should not determine what should be done or how it should be done from the perspective of the donor of those funds.

Many people get together because they share some common problem and they seek to alleviate this problem through collaboration. It may be as simple as older people getting together to exercise, do tai chi, or jog in the hope of warding off heart attacks, or it may be as serious as the parents of disabled children getting together to share their responsibilities, to learn from each other, and to support each other.

http://dx.doi.org/10.3362/9781780449081.004

Such a desire for collaboration may also be more of a one-off association, when, for instance, neighbours help each other in an emergency of fire or flooding. The reason for the association is a shared problem and a belief that collaboration and sharing is going to be advantageous to all members of the group. Change is not the chief motivation, but something more like mutual help. Such mutual help may be more formalized – as in mutual irrigation associations, savings and credit clubs, and marching societies – and one motivation may be cultural: to continue practices based in traditions that most people agree should not disappear, and that require a commitment of time and energy to keep alive.

There is often a feeling of optimism, self-congratulation, and self-praise for and by people who associate in such ways; this is worthwhile, does not harm anyone, and produces valuable social capital. We should not ignore, however, the possibilities of social tension and harm that may come from such associations. Husbands and wives may each complain that the other spends too much time at their club meetings and neglects their family responsibilities, for example.

A third group of people get together because their shared problems are very burdensome and they feel that 'something ought to be done about it'. They share a problem and together feel that it is within their power to improve the situation and address that problem. Thus, women coping with domestic violence do not merely share their problem with each other, but they associate in order to convince men not to be abusive, or to motivate the police to do something about the violence. Another example is new arrivals in large cities from the countryside who work together to build shanty towns, knowing that no one will help them but themselves.

Whatever the topic around which the group of people coalesces, the dynamics of starting a CSO are similar all over the world. Box 4.1 describes the voluntary sector in the United Kingdom.

Box 4.1 The voluntary sector

The voluntary sector is not in any way homogeneous. It encompasses the small group of local women coming together to support each other through a miscarriage, and international agencies such as Save the Children or Greenpeace; groups with annual incomes ranging from a few pounds to many millions; groups which are purely voluntary, with no paid workers, and others with hundreds of employees; groups committed to collective and cooperative working arrangements and those with rigid hierarchies; groups ranging politically from far right to far left – and everything in between.

It includes groups which primarily provide a service, those which primarily campaign, and those which do both; groups engaged in research or action or both. And it covers a huge range of sectors: arts, children, disability, education, elderly, employment, environment, health, hobbies, housing, human rights, peace, prison reform, sport, welfare, and dozens of others.

Box 4.1 The voluntary sector (*continued*)

The voluntary sector includes **charities** – organisations whose objects are wholly and exclusively charitable, which may or may not be registered with the Charity Commission or similar regulatory body – as well as many thousands of campaigning, self-help and other organisations which legally are defined as not being charitable despite being 'good causes'.

Historically the sector has at least five separate roots: philanthropy and the desire to help people who are 'less fortunate'; enhancing local communities through mutual aid and self-help; the desire to improve conditions through political and economic action; the desire to take on public services provided by the public or private sectors; and the simple reality of shared interests. While these overlap, different organisational histories can lead to significant differences in how organisations approach their work.

What all voluntary organisations have in common is that they are set up on a **non-profit** or **not-for-profit** basis. Despite what this sounds like, they *can* make a profit or surplus, but there will be a constitutional limit on how much (if any) of the organisation's profits or surplus can be distributed to its members or governing body (management committee/board) members. The constitution will require all profits or surplus, or any left over after the permitted distribution, to be reinvested in the organisation or used for the organisation's constitutional purposes.

The **not-for-profit** concept is gaining increasing attention, as more and more organisations become **social enterprises** or **community businesses** – organisations that earn all or most of their income through trading (charging for their goods or services). They may do this by entering into contracts with (rather than receiving grants from) public sector bodies, or they may charge their clients or service users, or they may sell goods produced by the people the organisation is set up to work with (for example, an organisation set up to work with disabled people which earns its income by selling goods produced by those people). One of the most significant shifts in the voluntary sector in recent years has been the move away from dependence on grants and donations and towards income generation through social enterprise.

Source: reprinted with permission from Adirondack, 2006

Mutual benefit organizations

In all these examples, the individual citizens themselves benefit from the effort that they put into social activities or sharing problems that they all suffer from. They are committing their energy and time to address – and hopefully solve – problems they are all facing. It is likely that such activities will be self-financed by those involved, and they will probably be managed in a participatory manner with officials appointed from the members of the group. These are mutual benefit organizations, where individuals work together to benefit themselves at the same time as they benefit other members of the group.

If such people are seen by other members of society as doing very valuable work that is admirable, is solving society's problems, and is complementing government activities, it may well be that they will be helped by citizens or by the government with funds, non-financial resources such as land, and access to credit. Also, it may be that such organizations will move to become a different kind of organization that seeks these kinds of support, and this will require fundraising, bank accounts, reporting on their activities, and more formal office holders. This is often the case with youth clubs – and Hollywood is full of stories of young people who are actually or potentially delinquent getting together to effect some activity in order to improve themselves.

Public benefit organizations

More common in development, however, are associations that have been started because individuals believe change needs to take place, and where this change is not to improve their own lives but to improve the lives of others who are considered to have a problem. These are public benefit organizations. They involve outsiders' perceptions of poverty and powerlessness in a particular group and their ideas of what should be done to improve the situation.

This gets much more complicated because of three difficult questions.

Who decides who is in need of help?

While few would object to efforts to improving conditions for people with disabilities or orphans, or to the motivations of people who want to do this, there are many more disputed targets of well-motivated people. Should convicted prisoners be helped? Should drug addicts, prostitutes, people living with AIDS, landless people, refugees? On the face of it, morally and ethically motivated people will say yes to all of the above, but as soon as such help is mobilized, they have to consider those who may not be so enthusiastic about it.

Victims of crime may not be keen to help criminals, prostitutes may be prepared to manage their own lives without interference, landowners will see accommodating the landless as likely to impinge on their own livelihoods, and citizens of one country may be unhappy that refugees of a different culture are being resettled in their nation. Even the traditional subjects of outsiders' help, such as people with disabilities, may well say that they want to help themselves, and may distance themselves from those who claim to want to help them.

Who decides how they should be helped?

When a self-appointed person or group decides that they know what needs to be done for others they think of as needing help, the choice of what they plan to do is a minefield. Those who want to help orphans by building orphanages will be contested by those who want to start a fostering programme. Those who want to prevent HIV/AIDS by distributing condoms will be contested by those who consider that condom use will encourage immorality in the young. Those who want to help the landless may not be happy with landless people's own militant tactics to acquire land by force. Those who want to help refugees will be very aware that refugees are fleeing countries with terrible conditions, and that they cannot control those conditions. The choice of strategy for the well-intentioned organization is very complicated.

Who should support those who want to help others?

If the organization that has identified the cause or the problem it wants to address is able to collect funds itself and to decide how these funds should be spent, this is a question to be discussed by the self-identified funders and those identified by the funders as the recipients of their funds. If I, as a businessperson, have disposable income that I would like to use to help ex-political prisoners, then I need to talk to those I would like to help to ascertain what kinds of help they think are the most effective, and what help they would be prepared to receive from me, under what conditions. It is a dialogue, complicated by the fact that the object of the assistance is often in a very bad way and may be grateful for any help, and therefore is unlikely to negotiate with the donor.

If, however (and this is much more likely), an organization is motivated to help an identified group but does not have the funds it needs for its intended programmes itself, then it has to persuade others to give to the organization, so that it can give to others. This introduces a whole new dimension. The organization has to persuade people not only to give for the identified good cause, but also to be prepared to give to the organization as the likely custodian of donated funds and to believe that it will be responsible and accountable. If the donating public are people from your own country (as is often the case with the Red Cross or Red Crescent), there is one level of complexity; if the donating public are from another country (or are not even the public, but the government), the level of complexity is even greater.

These are some of the problems of public benefit organizations, which, as we have seen, do not help themselves but help people that they have decided are worth helping, and which are prepared to ask third parties to provide help through them. We are getting closer to developmental CSOs and the complications of seeking funding from foreign donors.

What sort of organization should you set up?

What this means from the perspective of well-meaning people who want to start a developmental CSO and make sure that it runs well and effectively is that you need to decide early on whether you aim to start:

- a membership-driven mutual benefit organization that will help you as well as the other members of the organization, and that will be managed by its members;
- a supporter-driven public benefit organization that will help people you have chosen to help, and who are agreeable to being helped, and that will be managed by a group formed from the supporters, perhaps with some representation of the targeted group.

Once you have decided that, you will also have to decide whether you are going to:

- use your mutually collected resources to run the organization and its programmes;
- run the organization using your existing resources;
- seek resources from the public in your own country to run the organization and its programmes;
- seek resources from the public in other people's countries;
- seek resources from the governments of other people's countries.

Increased formality

In most countries, an informal group of enthusiasts who want to become more effective and more professional in their ability to bring about change need to do two things:

1. Become a formal registered organization. In some cases, this is necessary in order to do basic things such as opening a bank account; in other cases, it is clear that the government uses formal registration as a way of monitoring the work of CSOs.
2. Develop a plan that will be communicated to other people and persuade them to support it (or at least, in the case of the government, make no objections to it).

Registration

The move from an informal group of enthusiasts (for a particular cause, or against a particular injustice) to a registered organization under law has both positive and negative sides.

Negative

- It sorts out the people who are serious about committing their time, energy, and possibly money to a cause from those who are interested but are not prepared for such a commitment. This may reduce the numbers of people involved.
- Depending on the law in your country, you may find that you are constrained from doing some of the things that you and your associates wanted to do, and are liable for some things that you were not so interested in doing – usually writing reports and seeking permissions.
- Again depending on the law in your country, you may find that some of your options for seeking resources (fundraising or income generation) are constrained.
- The governance structure that is required (with boards, management committees, membership rolls, and so on) may be time consuming and take you away from work that you feel is more important.

Positive

- Having a legal identity may impress people who you want to enrol in your association – they might consider you serious and not simply amateurs.
- You may be eligible for certain privileges (for instance you may be eligible for tax exemption).
- You may find that the media is prepared to give your organization and its particular cause coverage and access to publicity.

On the other hand, you may simply find that as soon as you achieve any size, there is no alternative except to be registered since this is required by the law of your country.

Once you have made a decision about registration, you will probably have to decide how to formalize your organization, what legal persona to adopt, and how (and on what terms) you are prepared to present yourself to possible donors. At the simplest level, you will need to open a bank account. In many countries, opening an organizational bank account (as opposed to a private one) involves some form of legal persona and constitution. Box 4.2 gives an example of a constitution.

While a person may be motivated to set up a CSO based on their passion for fighting corruption, for instance, he or she will find it useful and important to learn more about setting up a legal organization in order to carry out the work effectively.

All this is based on the assumption that whoever you are – a membership society of people with the same problem or a self-selected group that has identified an issue or cause that you consider very important – you have the commitment to give time and energy to this cause or problem or issue, and that you prefer to do so through a not-for-profit, non-governmental organization rather than through either the government or business, or through some of the interesting hybrid forms that are appearing, such as social entrepreneurship or cause-related investments.

What follows is a checklist for the issues that you have to think about when creating a constitution for your organization. This will make a collection of enthusiasts appreciate the complexities that are involved in establishing and running an organization.

Box 4.2 Checklist for creating a constitution

New groups need to create a constitution; established groups may want to change theirs or have to create a new one if they change their registered status.

Whether drawing up a constitution on its own or consulting a lawyer or specialist agency which can help with registration, it will help to think through these questions first:

Legal structure

Have you learned about the various types of legal structure and considered whether it is appropriate for the organisation to become one or another? Have you considered the advantages and disadvantages of the different structures?

Box 4.2 Checklist for creating a constitution (*continued*)

Objects

What is the main purpose of the organisation? Why has it been set up? What are the subsidiary purposes? What does the organisation hope to achieve or do? Why? Who are the organisation's activities, services, and facilities for? Who are they not for? Are they only available to members?

Powers

Which powers are normally included in a constitution for the legal structure that you have chosen, and which of them are appropriate for your organisation to include? Powers set out what you can do to achieve your objects, and might include employing staff; raising funds; investing surplus funds; borrowing money; renting, buying or disposing of property; setting up branches etc. If allowed, there should be a general power along the lines of 'power to do any lawful act necessary for the achievement of the objects'.

Membership

Should it be a membership association? Who should be members? Who should not be members? Are there different categories of individual membership, for example – full membership and associate membership? Who is eligible for each?

Can groups or organisations be members? What are the criteria for group (corporate) membership? How are groups represented? Are the representatives there to represent the views of the group, or in their own right?

Can staff be members?

How is membership approved or not approved? Can membership be terminated? How?

Should there be a category of co-opted members? Can co-opted members vote? (Co-opted members are people who are not regular members or may not be eligible for membership, who are invited to join because of their particular expertise, commitment or interest.)

Should there be a category of honorary member? Can honorary members vote? (Honorary members are 'names' like the Mayor, actors or other public figures who can lend prestige to an organisation.)

Subscriptions

Should there be a subscription? Should it just be a nominal amount, or enough to generate some income for the organisation? Should there be different rates for different types of members or for people who are unemployed? What about members who are unable to pay?

Who sets the subscription? When is it set? When is it due? What about people who do not pay by the deadline?

AGM and general meetings

When should the annual general meeting (AGM) be held? How long before the meeting must members be notified? Who is eligible to attend? What is the quorum? (A quorum is the minimum number of members required for the meeting to make decisions and transact business.) What if a meeting is 'inquorate' (not enough people for a quorum)?

Should general meetings (of all the membership) be held at specified intervals? What is the period of notice for general meetings? What is the quorum for general meetings? What if a meeting is inquorate? How are extra-ordinary (special) meetings called and what are the procedures for them?

What is the procedure for voting in elections at AGMs and general meetings? What is the procedure for voting on resolutions? Can the Chair vote? What happens if there is an equality of votes (a tie)?

Box 4.2 Checklist for creating a constitution (*continued*)

Officers

How should officers be elected? The possibilities are:

- Elect officers and management committee at the AGM. Officers become management committee members and are officers of the organisation and management committee.

- Elect organisation's officers and management committee at the AGM. The organisation's officers become management committee members, but the management committee elects its own officers (different from the organisation's officers).

- Elect management committee at the AGM. The management committee elects officers who are officers of the organisation and the management committee.

Who is eligible to stand for election as an officer? What officers are needed? What are the duties of officers? Can officers resign? How are vacancies filled?

Management committee

How many members should the management committee have? Will you set a fixed number? If not, will you set a minimum? If you set a minimum, do you also want to set a maximum? Who is eligible for nomination? Do management committee members have to attend a minimum number of meetings? Do they get asked to leave if they, for instance, miss three meetings in a row?

Should there be provision for co-opted members? Who will decide who is co-opted? Can co-opted members vote?

What about representatives of the government, the local authority or founders? Can they be management committee members? Can they vote?

What about representation from other organisations who are not themselves corporate members of the organisation? Can they vote?

Can staff be members of the management committee? Are they on as individuals or as staff representatives? Should the constitution say that staff are not entitled to vote on matters concerning their contracts of employment? (It is not good practice for committee members to vote on any contract in which they have a financial interest.)

If staff are not on the committee, can they attend committee meetings? All staff or only some? As individuals or as staff representatives? Can they participate in discussion, or only observe and speak when asked to do so?

If staff resign from their job should there be a fixed period (usually six months or a year) before they can become a management committee member?

How will the first management committee be chosen? How will subsequent committees be chosen?

How often should the management committee meet? Who calls the meetings? What period of notice is required? What is the quorum? What happens if a meeting is inquorate?

What is the procedure for voting at management committee meetings, for elections and for resolutions? Are management committee meetings open to other members of the organisation? Can they participate or only observe? Can the chair vote? What happens if there is an equality of votes?

Sub-committees

Should there be a specific provision for an executive committee, made up of officers? Should there be specific provision for standing (permanent) sub-committees, such as personnel, finance or development? Should there be provision for sub-committees to be established as needed? Who decides? (AGM, general meeting, or management committee?) How are sub-committee members chosen? Can non-members of the organisation be members of sub-committees? Can they vote?

Box 4.2 Checklist for creating a constitution (*continued*)

Amendment/dissolution

How can the constitution be changed?

Who can decide to wind up the organisation? What happens to the assets if the organisation has to be wound up?

Rules and standing orders

In addition to its constitution, an organisation may have other rules or standing orders which set out how meetings are to be run, how decisions are made, when and how subscriptions are set or other procedural matters. These rules should be kept with the constitution, and if necessary the appropriate section of the constitution should be cross-referenced to the rule.

Source: adapted with permission from Adirondack, 1989

References

Adirondack, S. (1989), *Just About Managing? A Guide to Effective Management for Voluntary Organisations and Community Groups*, 1st edn, London: London Voluntary Service Council.

Adirondack, S. (2006), *Just About Managing? Effective Management for Voluntary Organisations and Community Groups*, 4th edn, London: London Voluntary Service Council.

CHAPTER 5
Moving from a good idea to a well-planned programme

Making plans

Many civil society organizations (CSOs) are staffed by people who come from an activist background.The simplest (and some would say the best) CSOs will be those that show how concerned citizens have identified for themselves things which they consider need to be done in their locality, in their country, or in their world, and are prepared to try their best to do it through their own efforts. If they want to persuade other people to support their work, however, in order to achieve what they are concerned about and committed to, then they have to move to being an organization that others are prepared to support and to which the government of their country is prepared to give legal recognition. Such an organization is a non-government, not-for-profit professional development agency.

This is likely to be an organization with principles that it will apply (such as participation, integrity, transparency, and accountability); with good systems and structures that provide for hiring, paying, training, and developing staff; with the structures necessary for planning, resourcing, implementing, and monitoring projects and programmes; with the ability to communicate its aims and purposes to the public; and with the ability to show government, the public, the media, and international development organizations the quality of the work that it does.

Beyond these immediate competences, the organization will also need to learn how to partner with other organizations, how to listen to their suggestions, and how to build joint and networked commitment. Finally – and increasingly – there will be a need to learn how to work with the government (particularly local government) as more and more government institutions become operational, and how to lobby or conduct advocacy for change in existing policies and practices. It is possible that your organization will find that it must adopt a strategy of trying to get government to support the changes it desires, or holding government responsible for changes that have not been implemented. This makes for a different kind of organization from one that effects change itself.

There are two basic kinds of skill needed:

1. skills in designing programmes so that you have viable and realistic ways of achieving your objectives and changing the world (or your bit of the world);
2. skills in running an organization so that the organization supports and bolsters your programmes – and, unless you are planning an organization that will exist for only a short time and with very limited objectives, skills in sustaining your organization and your programmes over time.

http://dx.doi.org/10.3362/9781780449081.005

Getting more serious about planning

The process by which an organization can move from being a group of enthusiastic people who have what they consider good ideas to improve the situation in their country to being an organization with a clear programme that has some chance of *being effective* and *getting results* (and which, moreover, is likely to get *commitment* and *enthusiasm* from its members or followers, and *support* from those in a position to pay for the costs of the programme) should go through the following steps:

1. Get clear about the problem you are trying to address.
2. Imagine or envision a future state in 20 years' time in which the problem has been overcome – to inspire you to undertake the programme.
3. Plan your organization's mission, i.e. the kind of work that your organization might do in the next five to 10 years to move towards your long-term vision.
4. Think through your strategy, i.e. the best way for your organization to carry out its mission and the best use of the resources you have or can access.
5. Make a serious plan for your programme (a set of long-term activities) or project (shorter-term activities).

Let us look at these one by one.

Slogans into problems

It is likely that a general agreement about the problems you want to address has already been reached by the supporters of your organization, but this will often be understood simplistically – and in the form of a slogan. It is important, however, to think through the problem and consider it from the perspective of the situation of your country, and the situation of your organization. When you do this in a systematic way, you may well refine your understanding of the problem and get a clearer idea of how you are situated to do something about it.

There are many structured ways of doing this – please take a look at Figure 5.1 as an example.

Let us start with some examples of specific problems that might have captured the imagination of your group and kindled their enthusiasm for doing something. The choice will probably be a product of your stakeholders' experience, their political perspectives, and their own interests.

These examples are basically slogans that are great for generating enthusiasm, but that lack the analysis needed before they can become the basis for a project which is going to have an impact. The slogans illustrate the issues that may have brought people together in your CSO in order to do something they consider useful. They are followed (in italics) by a slightly more nuanced explanation of the slogan.

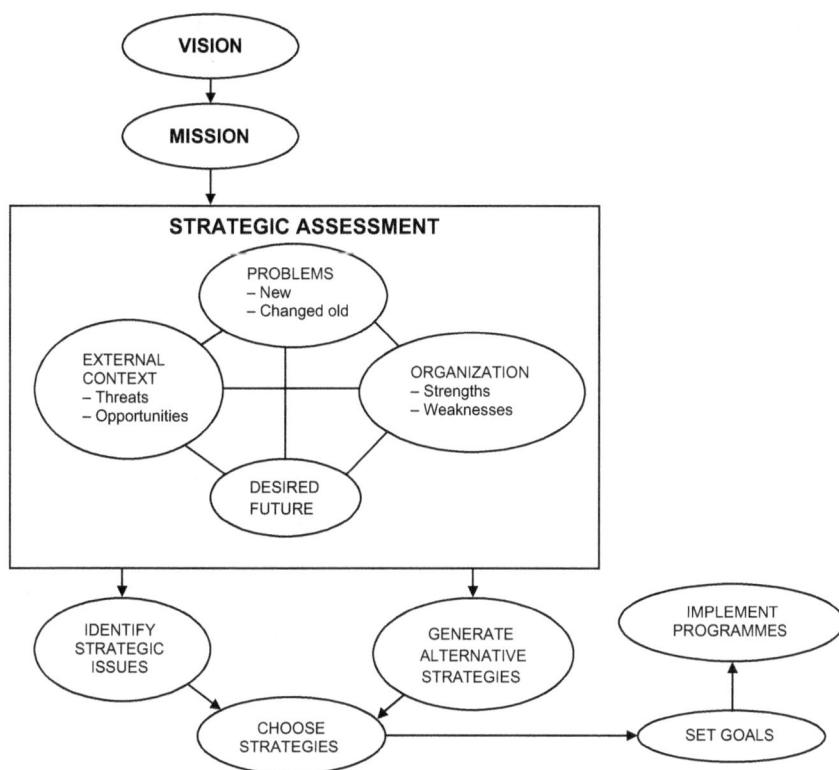

Figure 5.1 Overview of the strategy formulation process
Source: adapted by Richard Holloway from materials prepared by the Society for Participatory Research in Asia appearing in Covey et al, 1989

1. Stop the tribal fighting!
    Stop regular warfare and violence because of disputes over land and cattle.
2. Stop cutting trees!
    Combat excessive firewood cutting or charcoal production and prevent soil erosion.
3. Fair price for farmers' products!
    Reduce the exploitation of poor farmers by extortionate middlemen.
4. Stop illegal imports!
    Make sure that foreign imports pay taxes, not bribes to customs officers, so that local producers can compete.

Problem analysis

To move beyond slogans and into a well-considered programme or project, your organization has to think through what it wants to do and how it can do it. There are two very good tools to help this process: a SWOT analysis and a problem tree analysis. Both require an experienced facilitator to work with your organization's stakeholders.

SWOT analysis

SWOT stands for Strengths, Weaknesses, Opportunities, and Threats. With this exercise, a facilitator works with the organization's stakeholders to get ideas about the organization from each of these perspectives, and to brainstorm answers to the following questions:

- What are my organization's strengths?
- What are my organization's weaknesses?
- What are the opportunities for my organization (in the world in which we want to work)?
- What are the threats to my organization (in the world in which we want to work)?

The answers to these questions are displayed in the form of a four-part diagram, as shown below.

Strengths	Weaknesses
Opportunities	Threats

Problem tree analysis

Another valuable way of getting clarity about the problems you want to work on is to create a 'problem tree'. Here, a facilitator works with the organization's stake holders firstly to agree about the world in which the problem exists, and then to seek ideas about problems from the participants. These are usually written on cards that are then displayed and agreed by the participants. After eliminating cards that overlap and say the same thing, the facilitator tries to tease out:

1. the core problem – which is drawn as the trunk of the tree;
2. the causes of the problem – which are drawn as the roots of the tree;
3. the effects of the problem – which are drawn as the branches of the tree.

The facilitator works with the participants to find the logical links – which causes are allied, and which effects are the product of others.

At the end of these two exercises, the stakeholders of an organization will be very much clearer about the problem they are hoping to work on, and how they might design a programme or project to make a difference.

Refining slogans into problems

Here are examples of how slogans may be refined into a problem that can be worked on.

Slogan	Stop the tribal fighting!
Problem	There is ongoing violent conflict over land and cattle.
Slogan	Stop cutting trees!
Problem	There is a lack of firewood and increasing soil erosion.
Slogan	Fair price for farmers' products!
Problem	Farmers remain poor because middlemen do not give them a fair farm-gate price for their produce.
Slogan	Stop illegal imports!
Problem	Local producers are harmed by cheap foreign products being imported and by import taxes being avoided by the payment of bribes to customs officers.

The next step in the process is to try to imagine what the world would look like if you were successful in overcoming this problem.

A vision statement

The CSO should have a vision of the world it would like to see in the future – when the problem they are concerned about has been overcome. A serious NGO should not do one thing today, another thing tomorrow, and a third thing the day after that. It should think seriously about what is important to it, and the kind of world it would like to help create in its own country. A facilitator can help the organization's stakeholders think about their own vision for the world.

The vision should be of the ideal world that the CSO would like to see in 15 to 20 years' time. It may not be able to achieve that vision easily, but the vision is a guide for the direction in which it would like to move. The vision reflects the dreams the CSO has about the future reality it would like to see.

As examples, the CSO may have a vision of a world in 15 to 20 years' time in which:

1. all land and cattle disputes are settled peacefully;
2. all hillsides are covered in trees that provide regular firewood and there is no soil erosion;
3. all farmers get a fair price for their crops;
4. all goods are imported in accordance with the law.

Let us see how this moves on from the problem statement.

Slogan	Stop the tribal fighting!
Problem	There is ongoing violent conflict over land and cattle.
Vision	All land and cattle disputes are settled peacefully.

Slogan	Stop cutting trees!
Problem	There is a lack of firewood and increasing soil erosion.
Vision	All hillsides are covered in trees that provide regular firewood and there is no soil erosion.

Slogan	Fair price for farmers' products!
Problem	Farmers remain poor because middlemen do not give them a fair farm-gate price for their produce.
Vision	All farmers get a fair price for their crops.

Slogan	Stop illegal imports!
Problem	Local producers are harmed by cheap foreign products being imported and by import taxes being avoided by the payment of bribes to customs officers.
Vision	All goods are imported in accordance with the law.

An organization needs a vision statement so that its long-term goal is clear – a future state towards which the organization is driving. The vision is an expression of the ideals of the organization which it hopes to achieve within a generation. It is important for the organization to have a vision so that it keeps its focus when there may be many forces pushing it in other directions. This is particularly true when an organization comes under pressure due to the availability of funds.

If an organization has a vision of, for instance, a society without corruption within 20 years, or mothers bearing children safely by 2050, or self-reliance in rice in two generations, then it should think twice before it responds to opportunities to get involved in disaster relief or gender equity. Such activities may be very important, but they lead you away from the original reason for starting the organization and the original vision of the organization. If the organization is going to attract people and support for the main issue or cause that was its basis, it should stay true to its original vision.

However, a vision is only a starting point for building and maintaining an effective organization. There are many ways in which a single vision can be pursued, and plenty of scope for many different ways of trying to reach the desired future state.

The next level of activity is the mission.

Your mission

Most NGOs are committed to changing some aspect of the present social, physical, or economic situation. They have identified something that they consider is not right, and they are committed to changing the situation for the better. Many and varied are the things that possibly need to be improved, reformed, or changed.

For instance, NGOs see a particular problem that they want to overcome and they intend to base their activities on overcoming that problem. This was the reason for the original founders of the organization to come together.

Over time, however, they may identify a further problem that they had not considered before – such as the epidemic of HIV/AIDS – and they may decide they should also address that problem. Or a donor, impressed by the work they have done in one field, may offer them funding to work in a field that was not part of their original idea. They may find themselves doing a number of things without a clear direction, carrying out any activity that they consider important and for which they may get support.

To avoid such problems, NGOs should think long term about the kind of work they want to do and the kind of world they want to see in the future. This is the purpose of the visioning exercise. Agreeing on such a vision is useful because it binds together an organization, clarifies its ideals, and gives it momentum and commitment. It also helps to explain to others what the NGO stands for.

An organization, however, needs a more specific and clearer purpose for its activities than a vision, and this is where the mission comes in.

The mission statement

While the CSO needs to have a vision of the world it would like to see in 15 to 20 years' time, it also needs to have a much tighter idea of what it is going to do this year – and what it is not going to do. It needs to have a clear statement of its 'mission' – that is, its *reason for existing*. The statement of the mission (at most one paragraph, or 50 words) gives the reason for the organization's existence, and describes how the organization is going to try to achieve its vision.

A mission can be described as the purpose of the organization, using language that says what you want to do ('This organization's mission is to do xxx').

For each of the examples given earlier, we can think of a possible mission statement that tells us what the organization is going to do to try to achieve its vision. Let us look at the problem and the vision and now create a mission that clarifies what the organization plans to do, with whom, and over what period of time.

Slogan	Stop the tribal fighting!
Problem	There is ongoing violent conflict over land and cattle.
Vision	All land and cattle disputes are settled peacefully.
Mission	The purpose (mission) of this organization is, over the next five years, to mediate between warring parties (xx and yy) in zz area of the country so that disputes are settled without violence.
Slogan	Stop cutting trees!
Problem	There is a lack of firewood and increasing soil erosion.
Vision	All hillsides are covered in trees that provide regular firewood and there is no soil erosion.
Mission	The purpose (mission) of this organization is, over the next five years, to persuade the people who live in the hilly areas of our country to plant trees and to reduce clear cutting of trees for firewood.

Slogan	Fair price for farmers' products!
Problem	Farmers remain poor because middlemen do not give them a fair farm-gate price for their produce.
Vision	All farmers get a fair price for their crops.
Mission	The purpose (mission) of this organization is, over the next five years, to help farmers in xx region to negotiate a fair price for their produce with their buyers, and to increase their income.
Slogan	Stop illegal imports!
Problem	Local producers are harmed by cheap foreign products being imported and by import taxes being avoided by the payment of bribes to customs officers.
Vision	All goods are imported in accordance with the law.
Mission	The purpose (mission) of this organization is, over the next five years, to reduce bribery, which prevents import tax payments due at customs points xx and yy, and to help local producers compete with foreign imports.

These examples are a much more focused statement of how the organization intends to achieve its vision, and clarify what the organization will do, and will not do, where it will do it, who it will work with, and over what period of time.

The mission is the instrument for keeping an organization focused and effective, and for keeping it from being disorganized and all over the place. The mission is also the most prominent public communication about your organization. It should be written in your brochure – and perhaps included in your letterhead – and known by heart by your staff. It is the reason for your existence as a CSO.

Another important thing about a mission statement is that, as well as telling your staff and the public about the purpose of your organization, it also tells people what is *not* the purpose of the organization, so that they do not approach you with irrelevant requests. The mission statement is the way of focusing your organization and making sure that everyone is working towards the same purpose.

The strategy or choice of options

An organization may be clear about its vision for the future (for example, *All hillsides covered in trees and no soil erosion*) and it may be clear about its reason for existing (for example, *to reduce soil erosion and reforest the hills*), but many organizations have not thought intensively about what is the best way for them to carry out their mission – what is the best use of the resources they have or can access. What this means is that few of them have a clear *strategy*.

A strategy is how you use your human, physical, financial, and knowledge resources to pursue your mission. A strategy helps you to think about:

- the nature of the problem you are trying to solve;
- the opportunities and difficulties that exist in the world in which you are working;
- the strengths and weaknesses of your organization.

We can think about a strategy that is suitable for an organization with an agreed vision and mission. However, there may be many different strategies to achieve your mission, not just one.

Let us look at the second example. If the organization's mission is, over the next five years, to persuade the people who live in the hilly areas of the country to plant trees and to reduce clear cutting of trees for firewood, then that organization has a number of possible ways to carry out its mission. It could:

- hold educational classes for village people on the dangers of soil erosion;
- run training programmes for villagers in contour ploughing and creating small bunds;
- try to persuade traditional leaders to tell their people not to burn the grass;
- distribute seeds to villagers for quick-growing trees;
- identify one area and work to make a model of good anti-erosion practice, and bring others to see it;
- hold public education campaigns on radio and television about the dangers of soil erosion.

These are all possible strategies – different ways to achieve the same purpose or mission.

From all these alternatives, the CSO would choose one or two of these strategies (i.e. ways of working) because:

- they fit the skills and interests of the CSO's staff;
- they have a good chance of being accepted by the people;
- they have a good chance of success;
- they fit the financial resources that the CSO can attract.

The strategy needs to fit the real world – the real world of local participants, your CSO's capacity, government policies, and the available finance. Your strategy will be the way in which you choose to carry out your mission in the real world.

Let us look at each of our other examples and see the strategies that might be applied.

Slogan	Stop the tribal fighting!
Problem	There is ongoing violent conflict over land and cattle.
Vision	All land and cattle disputes are settled peacefully.
Mission	The purpose (mission) of this organization is, over the next five years, to mediate between warring parties (xx and yy) in zz area of the country so that disputes are settled without violence.

Possible strategies	• Train mediators to work in volatile areas. • Offer training to traditional leaders. • Set up a rapid reaction team to try to stop fighting before it gets too serious. • Try to confiscate weapons. • Set up youth clubs for potential young warriors.
Slogan	Fair price for farmers' products!
Problem	Farmers remain poor because middlemen do not give them a fair farm-gate price for their produce.
Vision	All farmers get a fair price for their crops.
Mission	The purpose (mission) of this organization is, over the next five years, to help farmers in xx region to negotiate a fair price for their produce with their buyers, and to increase their income.
Possible strategies	• Help develop a farmers' cooperative to bypass the middlemen and sell to end users. • Help local farmers to diversify into high-value crops and help them to find markets. • Build bulk storage units and train farmers in marketing. • Lobby local government to fix minimum prices for crops.
Slogan	Stop illegal imports!
Problem	Local producers are harmed by cheap foreign products being imported and by import taxes being avoided by the payment of bribes to customs officers.
Vision	All goods are imported in accordance with the law.
Mission	The purpose (mission) of this organization is, over the next five years, to reduce bribery, which prevents import tax payments due at customs points xx and yy, and to help local producers compete with foreign imports.
Possible strategies	• Educate government officials about the effect that corruption has on the income of local producers. • Set up a customs monitoring unit to identify corruption. • Help local producers to form associations to protest against the behaviour of customs officers. • Train police and a local unit of the anti-corruption commission to tackle local corruption.

The programme and the project

When you have decided on your vision, your mission, and your strategy, then you need to get down to the serious planning of your programme (a set of long-term activities) or project (a set of shorter-term activities). Your programme or project will need:

- a time frame;
- the result you hope will be achieved by the end of the programme or project by your CSO as well as by others working in the same field;
- the results that your CSO on its own is committed to achieve;
- the activities that you will undertake to achieve these results;
- the budget that is needed to carry out this programme or project.

Because there is always a danger of over-optimism, and of people thinking they have been successful when it may not be the case, it is also important to think about signs or indicators of success for the project. How will you know that you have succeeded? Your programme or project will also need:

- indicators of success, and how they will be measured.

For example: 1) What reduction in the number of deaths has there been? 2) What changes in farm-gate prices have taken place? 3) What increases in revenue for the customs department have been received?

Assumptions and risks

Finally, it is very important to think about what others have to do if the programme is going to be a success. What assumptions are you making about other people's actions? And what assumptions are you making about the world that you do not control?

It is unlikely that your CSO can do everything by itself to make the programme a success. It will also need to have contributions from other people. And there will also be risks involved. You need to think about all these aspects in advance to make sure that these contributions will take place and these risks are managed. For instance, if one of your activities is educational classes in the village, you will need to have the agreement of the village head. If you do not have that agreement, the programme will fail. So take a note in your planning that you need the village head to agree.

If you are going to be working with a government agency, and you come from a CSO, you need to think about whether the government agency will be approachable by a CSO and, if so, how and by whom. This becomes an important point that you need to include in your planning.

Using a log frame

Let us now take the four examples of slogan, vision, mission, and strategy, and design possible programmes or projects that will include the objectives, the activities, and the assumptions.

We can put these ideas into a diagram called a log frame (or logical framework analysis). A log frame is a very common diagrammatic shorthand for planning that many people will understand and look for in your organization, as a sign that you have thought through the elements necessary for implementing a project or programme. In each case, let us look at the elements of the project or programme and then suggest a log frame.

Note that these are suggestions. If you do not agree with all the elements, or you have others to add, please do so. The text is to illustrate the kind of thing that you need to think about.

The reason why a log frame is called a 'logical framework' is that there is some logic between the different levels. If an activity is done properly and succeeds, then it will lead to the achievement of the next level (usually called the output). This, in turn, will contribute to the next level (usually called the purpose). The accomplishment of this will then lead to the organization's long-term vision or goal being achieved.

Let us look at the first example.

Slogan	Stop the tribal fighting!
Problem	There is ongoing violent conflict over land and cattle.
Vision	All land and cattle disputes are settled peacefully.
Mission	The purpose (mission) of this organization is, over the next five years, to mediate between warring parties (xx and yy) in zz area of the country so that disputes are settled without violence.
Possible strategies	• Train mediators to work in volatile areas. • Offer training to traditional leaders. • Use a rapid reaction team to try to stop fighting before it gets too serious. • Try to confiscate weapons. • Set up youth clubs for potential young warriors.
Possible programme or project objectives	• Successfully train and deploy cadres of mediators. • Train local leaders, who effectively reduce violence. • Set up a rapid reaction team when violence flares up. • Organize the collection of guns and put them beyond use. • Organize an alternative to fighting for young people.
Possible activities	• Train mediators. • Set up listening posts to be informed of possible trouble. • Identify local leaders interested in reducing violence. • Bring together important stakeholders (police, traditional leaders, women's groups, religious groups). • Negotiate the idea of handing in guns with important stakeholders. • Arrange sports competitions.
Possible assumptions	• There is not an important ongoing feud that has to be settled before anything else is possible. • There is not a powerful drought that exacerbates cattle theft. • Political leaders are not using tribal warfare for political purposes.

In this case, if we choose the strategy of setting up youth clubs for young warriors, then our activity would be to arrange sports competitions, and these, if successful, could lead to the objective of an alternative to fighting for young people. This, in turn, may lead to the purpose of the work, which is to settle disputes without violence. And all of this has the possibility of working, providing that the youth are not encouraged to fight by other parties as part of a larger political plan.

Let us look at another scenario.

Slogan	Fair price for farmers' products!
Problem	Farmers remain poor because middlemen do not give them a fair farm-gate price for their produce.
Vision	All farmers get a fair price for their crops.

Mission	The purpose (mission) of this organization is, over the next five years, to help farmers in xx region to negotiate a fair price for their produce with their buyers, and to increase their income.
Possible strategies	• Help develop a farmers' cooperative to bypass the middlemen and sell to end users. • Help local farmers to diversify into high-value crops and help them to find markets. • Build bulk storage units and train farmers in marketing. • Lobby local government to fix minimum prices for crops.
Possible programme or project objectives	• Establish competent and functioning farmers' producer cooperatives. • Farmers cultivate a variety of new, high-value crops. • Farmers sell their new crops to buyers other than the traditional ones. • Small producers bulk up their produce in collaboration with each other. • Local government sets minimum price levels for local crops and enforces their implementation.
Possible activities	• Organize training for farmers in cooperative practices. • Introduce extension services for new crops. • Find buyers for new crops. • Organize depots where farmers can bring their produce and buyers can collect the produce. • Organize local farmers' associations to lobby local legislators for minimum price levels.
Possible assumptions	• Local legislators are in cahoots with local buyers and want to keep prices low. • Local farmers have had bad experiences in the past of government-organized cooperatives. • There are no serious outbreaks of pests to destroy the crops.

In this case, if we chose the strategy of building farmers' cooperatives, then we would need the activity of organizing training for farmers in cooperative practices, which, if successful, would lead to the objective of successful cooperatives functioning effectively. This would contribute to the project purpose of farmers increasing their income, and contribute to the vision or goal of all farmers getting a fair price for their crops, with the assumption that the farmers would not be affected by a serious outbreak of crop disease.

And let us look at the last scenario. Can you follow the logic? Does it make sense?

Slogan	Stop illegal imports!
Problem	Local producers are harmed by cheap foreign products being imported and by import taxes being avoided by the payment of bribes to customs officers.
Vision	All goods are imported in accordance with the law.
Mission	The purpose (mission) of this organization is, over the next five years, to reduce bribery, which prevents import tax payments due at customs points xx and yy, and to help local producers compete with foreign imports.
Possible strategies	• Educate government officials about the effect that corruption has on the income of local producers.

	• Set up a customs monitoring unit to identify corruption. • Help local producers to form associations to protest against the behaviour of customs officers. • Train police and a local unit of the anti-corruption commission to tackle local corruption.
Possible programme or project objectives	• Government officials with integrity, who understand the damaging effects of corruption. • A functioning and effective corruption monitoring unit. • Functioning and effective associations of local producers who are ready to seek redress from corrupt officials. • An active and functioning local arm of the national anti-corruption agency.
Possible activities	• Undertake training courses in integrity for government officials. • Set up a corruption monitoring unit. • Set up associations of local producers and train them to demand accountability from government. • Lobby for a local branch of the national anti-corruption agency.
Possible assumptions	• Local government is not in cahoots with the customs officials. • Government anti-corruption officials can be bribed to ignore what they should do.

Monitoring

Monitoring, when closely allied to planning, means you will check that what you planned to do is actually being done, and that it is having the effects that you hoped it would have.

In order to do this, you need to think in advance of what would be the signs of success at each stage of your activities, objectives, and purpose. Once you have a clear idea of what would be the signs of success, you can check to see whether you are achieving these.

This table provides an example.

	Objectives	Indicators of success	Assumptions and risks
Purpose or mission	To reduce soil erosion and reforest the hills	Reduction in soil erosion and greater forest cover on hills	Good rainfall
Output of objective	5,000 seeds distributed to each of five villages in badly eroded areas and planting techniques taught	4,000 well-growing trees in one year's time	Village head will support the programme
Activities	1. Collect seeds 2. Distribute them to villagers 3. Demonstrate planting techniques 4. Agree eroded land for re-planting by villagers		Villagers will work voluntarily, not demanding pay

Examples of log frames

Here are four log frames to look at. We have chosen from the possible options to make a coherent plan, but one that still has plenty of detail to be added – particularly the indicators of success and the means of verification, which is where you can find the information to verify that the indicators of success are true. Obviously, you would need to think this through in your CSO and decide which option makes most sense.

We have brought the CSO from a slogan to a log frame that can be shown to other people as evidence that you have thought logically about the problems, the objectives, the outcomes, the outputs, and the activities.

	Objectives	Indicators of success	Means of verification	Assumptions
Goal	All land and cattle disputes are settled peacefully.			• There is not an important ongoing feud that has to be settled before anything else is possible.
Purpose	The purpose (mission) of this organization is, over the next five years, to mediate between warring parties (xx and yy) in zz area of the country so that disputes are settled without violence.			
Output	• Cadres of mediators successfully trained and deployed. • Local leaders trained and effectively reducing violence.			• There is not a powerful drought that exacerbates cattle theft. • Political leaders are not using tribal warfare for political purposes.
Activity	• Train mediators. • Set up listening posts to be informed of possible trouble. • Identify local leaders interested in reducing violence.			

	Objectives	Indicators of success	Means of verification	Assumptions
Goal	All farmers get a fair price for their crops.			• Local legislators are not in cahoots with local buyers and want to keep prices low.
Purpose	The purpose (mission) of this organization is, over the next five years, to help farmers in xx region to negotiate a fair price for their produce with their buyers, and to increase their income.			• Local farmers have had bad experiences in the past of government-organized cooperatives.
Output	• Establish competent and functioning farmers' producer cooperatives. • Farmers cultivate a variety of new, high-value crops. • Farmers sell their new crops to buyers other than the traditional ones.			• There are no serious outbreaks of pests to destroy the crops.

(continued)

	Objectives	Indicators of success	Means of verification	Assumptions
Activity	• Organize training for farmers in cooperative practices. • Introduce extension services for new crops. • Find buyers for new crops.			

	Objectives	Indicators of success	Means of verification	Assumptions
Goal	All goods are imported in accordance with the law.			• Local government is not in cahoots with the customs officials.
Purpose	The purpose (mission) of this organization is, over the next five years, to reduce bribery, which prevents import tax payments due at customs points xx and yy, and to help local producers compete with foreign imports.			• Government anti-corruption officials can be bribed to ignore what they should do.
Output	• Government officials with integrity, who understand the damaging effects of corruption. • A functioning and effective corruption monitoring unit.			
Activity	• Undertake training courses in integrity for government officials. • Set up an anti-corruption commission monitoring unit.			

If you have followed this process, you have moved from a group of enthusiasts who have a single aim or goal, through to people who have thought through the difficulties and the possibilities of trying to achieve their purpose in the real world, and who have shown themselves able to make a plan that they can encourage others to support.

The next chapter looks at who you might get to support your plan.

Reference

Covey, J., Brown, D. and Leach, M. (1989) *Managing Organisation Change: A Module for Facilitators and Trainers*, Boston, MA: Institute for Development Research.

CHAPTER 6

How can you mobilize resources for your civil society organization?

Most civil society organizations (CSOs) will immediately think of seeking foreign funding for their activities. This book will suggest ways of seeking foreign funding, but it will also point out the limitations of foreign funding, and the need for CSOs to consider alternatives to it, particularly domestic funding. It is important to appreciate the range of funds available in the global North and South – from the gift economy, government, and the market.

Foreign funding

Foreign funding, in theory, is available to your CSO from a range of different institutions: any or all of international NGOs, international foundations, bilateral aid agencies, and multilateral development agencies. Some of these agencies are likely to have offices in your own country and this is obviously the place to start. Others do not have a local presence and need to be contacted through their head offices. You should discuss funding sources with other CSOs in your own country and follow up on their suggestions. In some cases, international organizations will have set up national grant-making bodies to spend their money for them.

There is a need for some realism, if not scepticism, in dealing with foreign donors. The best situation is where your organization and the foreign donor organization are united in a common desire to fight abuses in the field you have identified for your work, and decide to work together. Be aware, however, that foreign donors' actions do not always stem from simple altruism. They may be prepared to help your organization for a number of other reasons. You need to be aware of these since they may affect your relationship with them:

- a political decision in the donors' own country (and this decision may subsequently be reversed);
- a desire by the local representative to impress his or her head office;
- a desire by the local representative to expand his or her portfolio;
- a political signal to the government of your country;
- a desire to use up 'leftover' funding from some other project;
- an attempt by the organization to involve itself in some development 'fad' or fashion.

Try to assess the motivation of the donor you are dealing with. If you are satisfied with it, and you are clear that you want to raise foreign funding, then you need to make the approach. A CSO's ability to raise foreign funding

http://dx.doi.org/10.3362/9781780449081.006

depends on factors both internal and external to the organization. Let's start with the first.

Factors internal to the organization

These are questions the prospective foreign donor will ask about your CSO:

- Is the organization independent and non-partisan?
- Is the organization effective? What is its track record?
- Is the organization credible?
- Is the organization well managed?
- Does the organization have a clear idea of where it is going?
- Is the proposal clear and well written?
- Does the proposal provide all the information we need to know?
- Does the proposal reflect a planning process?

Factors external to the organization

These are questions that your CSO should be asking about the prospective donor:

- Is the donor interested in the subject of greatest concern to your CSO?
- Does the donor have funds available in your country?
- Does the donor usually provide funds in the amounts that you are asking for?
- Does the donor provide funds for the time periods you are asking for?
- Are you prepared for the rules and regulations of this particular donor?
- Does the donor have a good track record of keeping its word, delivering on time, and so on?
- Are you prepared to take money from this particular donor?

Limitations of foreign funding

Donors think in terms of projects – time-limited, specific activities with fixed budgets. You will almost certainly have to request support for the work that you want to do in terms of a project, even if what you really want is long-term budgetary support for your organization's programme, particularly when you are starting. It is very likely that a foreign donor will want to start small with a short-timescale project. This, if carried out successfully, will get you established, and you can build on the success to request more funds and more general programmatic funds.

Occasionally, you may find a donor who will be prepared to talk to you about the long-term sustainability of your organization – through, for example, an endowment or the gift of a building that could be used for your office and also be rented out to generate income for your organization. Be prepared to raise such issues, emphasizing the need for sustainability of your NGO. Such donors are rare, and are very unlikely to respond to your requests until they have some experience of working successfully with your CSO on shorter-term projects.

Be aware of the following factors that limit the attractiveness of foreign funding:

- International aid is fickle; it changes with political considerations in the donors' home country, and development 'fashions'. You may find that support is withdrawn or not renewed for factors unconnected to the success of your work.
- International aid comes as projects; this may not fit what you need, and you may find yourself having to twist and shape what you really want to do so that it fits donor options.
- International aid does not build up support for your CSO within your own country. It can make you vulnerable to accusations of being a stooge of a foreign government or organization.
- International aid generally does not help you become more self-reliant. It usually makes you dependent for your activities on resources that you cannot control. Most people would say that this is developmentally unsound. It is possible to get funding to build up self-reliance, and you should ask for this where possible (see later), but it is difficult.

Foreign non-funding support

Although it is foreign money that is normally the most attractive aspect of foreign development organizations, your CSO should also consider some of their important non-monetary aspects. These can include:

- technical help with the subject of concern of your CSO, through information, books, technical data, or people;
- solidarity – the readiness of foreign organizations to stand with you and back you by defending your work, affirming your commitment, publicizing your achievements, or helping you when you are attacked;
- links to other sources of help or information overseas;
- collaboration in pursuing information from their own country that has repercussions in your country.

Foreign companies

Increasingly, foreign businesses are open to proposals to help CSOs in the South. In most cases, this follows their expansion in setting up manufacturing plants in the South, and their desire to be recognized as good corporate citizens in your country, just as they try to be back in their own country. In some cases, local branches or affiliates are given the authority to use their promotions or advertising budget to help CSOs. In other cases, proposals have to be made to the headquarters of the company or the foundation that the company has set up. At a time of natural disaster, it is quite common for businesses to want to show that they are concerned about the situation.

Alternative resource mobilization

When we look beyond international funding to domestic sources of support, we must be clear that we are looking at all kinds of resources – not just money. For this reason, it is important to think of 'resource mobilization' and not just 'fundraising'. Part of these resources is volunteers; part is donations in kind; part is local goods and services, such as land or free vehicle maintenance; and part can be simply useful advice. Learning how to ask for and get various kinds of free goods and services locally is potentially much more important when you are looking for local resources. There are potential problems, however - see Box 6.1

Whether you are asking for money or other resources, you will find that the psychological dynamics change considerably when you are seeking resources in your own country. You will be trying to persuade your own countrymen and women, either personally or organizationally, to support your work – and this becomes a personal matter. This is quite a different situation from seeking funds from foreign donor organizations whose job it is to give out funds to CSOs in the South. Part of the psychological dynamics is that, in effect and in part, you will be asking local people or organizations to pay for the costs of your salaries, or your CSO's staff salaries, and some people see this as begging. Many people do not like to be seen as a beggar.

To be a successful fundraiser in your own country, it is very important to overcome this prejudice. You are not begging for money for yourself: you are offering people the opportunity to become involved in a cause that you believe in, and that you hope they will also believe in. If you strongly believe in, for instance, ridding your country of corruption, or preserving the environment, or making sure that human rights are respected, then you will be interested in providing your countrymen and women, in whatever way you come across them, with the opportunity to become involved in this noble cause. You are actually allowing them to do something concrete about a topic that may have excited them for many years, but about which they felt powerless.

Look at the variety of different ways you can mobilize resources locally. To some extent, this depends on your country's laws and regulations as well as its culture and the existing patterns of philanthropy. Different countries have different attitudes and habits about giving for public causes. It may be that in some countries part of your work will be to educate people about how they can support worthwhile causes through a local CSO because this is not something they have done before.

It is unfortunately true that, apart from making traditional contributions to religious and charitable good works, many people in the South do not see the need to raise money locally for development projects. Easy access to foreign aid has meant that many people feel this is the job of foreign funding, and that, if you work in this field, you should be asking those sources for money.

Asking the public for money (or other resources)

At its simplest, this would involve soliciting the general public for help through street collections or house-to-house collections, but it could also involve appeals for help to specific groupings of the public – via clubs, associations, or other membership groups. A specific version of this could be collecting from places of employment through agreed payroll donations. Some fundraising can also be done through events (sponsored walks, auctions, etc.). Do not forget that one very basic way of raising money is by selling membership in your organization.

Another way of fundraising is by providing some special service for which a price is paid, knowing that the funds will go to your organization. Such services could include special events with sponsored entertainment (concerts, parties, walks, or sports). Yet another way of asking for help from the general public is through targeted advertising in which your organization simply requests support for the work that it is doing via the media, or invites people to join the organization and, in doing so, pay a membership fee. The aim of a membership scheme, however, is not necessarily just to raise money; it could also be targeted at people who are interested in doing something to help your CSO more generally.

Many of these approaches require considerable numbers of volunteers to help organize them. They also require considerable expertise as it is easy to lose money in the process of trying to raise money, particularly when organizing events.

The other aspect of public fundraising is that, in the process of raising money, you will be announcing the existence of your organization, and sympathizers may well bring you information that is valuable for your work.

Asking the business sector for money (or other resources)

It is possible that the cause your CSO espouses would appeal to the business sector in your country, and businesses might be interested either in making a donation to your CSO or in sponsoring some event that will bring you income (as well as highlighting their own corporate identity). It may be that businesses would feel that their public identification with your CSO would be politically unwise, but they are still willing to help surreptitiously – perhaps with such useful items as furniture, second-hand computers, or the use of a building. Perhaps the most useful kinds of support that a business can give you are information pertinent to your cause and help with the running of your organization. A gift of the time of specialized people (lawyers, advertisers, artists, or accountants, for example) could be very valuable.

The CSO, of course, has to weigh up the possible benefits of help from the business sector with the disadvantages that may come from too close an association with a particular company. The company may be using the CSO to 'clean up' its name, but your CSO may find its public identification with the business unhelpful.

Asking government for money (or other resources)

Many CSOs feel that the government is part of the problem they are trying to overcome, and that the government is unlikely to be a source of help to a CSO. There are many possibilities, however, for collaboration with government, and dialogue can reveal areas in which both sides see such a collaboration as being in both their interests. Some of this will be in technical fields – the government, for instance, may be able to provide skilled vets for a goat-rearing programme – but some will also be in social development and human rights fields. Governments are not monolithic and it is possible that there are some parts of government that will be impressed by your CSO's track record and would like to support your work. They can help with contracts, which is probably not what your CSO wants, but do not ignore the possibility of them also helping with second-hand goods, property, and even land, as well as inside information (as they see it) about the subject with which you are concerned.

Just as with businesses, your CSO may think that any association with government is likely to be harmful to its own image. This will very much depend on the local circumstances in each country.

Generating your own income

Too often, thoughts about fundraising overshadow thoughts about fund-generating. Yet, many NGOs feel that ownership of a sustainable source of income in the form of a profit-making enterprise is one of the best ways to assure themselves of an income that is not compromised, that gives them a platform to publicize their movement, and that can ensure sustainability.

The difficulty comes in identifying an enterprise that is likely to make a profit and whose profits can be passed over to the work of the CSO. It is very easy to get involved in an intended money-making enterprise that not only does not make money but also sucks people, time, and money away from the real work of your CSO.

However, income *can* be generated from enterprises: either through those connected to the work of your CSO (books or reports for sale, commissioned research) or through enterprises that are unconnected (the sale of T-shirts or key rings, providing internet services, renting property, and so on). If you are fortunate enough to have members with definite business acumen, and if your CSO has the capital to invest, your CSO can go into any business that

---

Box 6.1 Problems and issues in alternative resource mobilization

1. Deciding to try to raise funds locally is a big decision for a local organization, particularly one that has previously been accustomed to raising funds from foreign donors. The biggest issue for such organizations is actually agreeing to undertake this method of resource mobilization and committing to making it work. It will require a strategic reorientation of the organization to include people responsible for membership, fundraising, and so on, and it will change the way you do business.
2. Another problem for many organizations is the worry that the fundraising and resource mobilization side of their work will divert the organization from its main role on the issues that it has identified. It is quite possible that the organization will put too much effort into running sponsored events, or selling T-shirts, to the detriment of its main mission.
3. A third problem is keeping on the right side of the law. In many countries the idea of a non-profit organization earning income for itself has no legal precedent, and such an organization may find itself paying tax like a for-profit business – to such an extent that trying to earn income no longer makes economic sense.
4. A fourth consideration is the worry about associating with for-profit businesses. All too frequently non-profit organizations feel that the image portrayed by such an association will reflect negatively on their organization. They are not happy to be associated with a profit-making enterprise.
5. Lastly, there are internal organizational problems. As your organization grows, it may need to hire staff dedicated to the fundraising and income generation side of things. Will they be paid the same as the people working on the main mission of the organization? Will they be under the same system of supervision? Such issues can divide an organization and cause all sorts of tensions that divert the organization from its main mission.

---

will make money, will not detract from the main work of the organization, and does not harm your image. It is important to remember, however, that running an enterprise to make money for your organization can end up harming the organization if the business takes up so much time that your original mission suffers.

One form of enterprise that is very attractive to CSOs is the investment business. If a CSO is successful in persuading a benefactor to give it a trust fund, or property, or stocks and shares, then the CSO can receive income in perpetuity from the investment of those funds or the renting of those properties (providing they are well managed) without needing further fundraising efforts. In Islamic countries, CSOs might seek to persuade Muslim donors to provide a *waqf* endowment.

Tax exemption

It is, of course, very helpful if your CSO can obtain from your country's government some form of tax-exempt status, which will allow it not to pay import duties, income tax, value-added tax or any other taxes in the country concerned. Such an exemption would mean that any money raised or generated would not be reduced through the payment of taxes.

The principle involved here is that your CSO is doing something useful for the government, something that the government would otherwise have to do itself (and use its own resources to do). Therefore, it is logical and sensible for the government to free the CSO from paying the taxes that would supply the government with the income to do this work itself.

However logical the case that the CSO can make may be, this issue is not one that will be decided on the basis of your CSO alone. Many CSOs can make the same argument, and the government policy on tax exemption for non-profit organizations with a social purpose is often complicated and has a long history. Your CSO will probably be best served by joining its efforts to those of other CSOs.

Making a proposal

Whether you are seeking funds internationally or locally, a common feature will be a good proposal. A proposal is simply a good argument that will persuade some individual or organization to help your organization. It needs to cover all the kinds of questions that a donor is likely to ask, and it needs to be clear, well presented, and logical. Do not forget that the donor may be a foreign agency, a local business, your government, a local club, or Mr and Mrs Smith down the street.

Many CSOs have been exposed to very complicated proposal application forms from foreign donors. It is good to get down to the essential elements of a proposal, which are:

1. Description: who you are, the problem your organization was established to solve, and what you have achieved to date.
2. Objectives: what you hope to accomplish, and what results you hope to achieve.
3. Methods: how you intend to achieve the stated objectives, and why you have chosen these methods.
4. Monitoring and evaluation: how you intend to evaluate the effectiveness of your work, in terms of both process and impact.
5. Money: what you need and how long for.
6. Funding strategy: how you intend to raise the funds required, and how you intend to continue after the present funding period is over.
7. Budget: the amounts of money you need broken down into capital and recurrent expenditure over the period requested. Make sure you include budget notes that explain why you need certain goods, or how the prices have been identified. Also make sure you include an allowance for inflation on multi-year projects, and an overhead rate or administrative fee.
8. A summary of all of the above on one page.

You may find the checklist of components of a proposal in Box 6.2 useful.

Box 6.2 Checklist of things to include in your proposal

1. Do you really believe in what you are doing and the value of the project?
2. Have you got a strategy?
3. Have you planned ahead?
4. Have you selected a good project that will appeal to that particular donor (if you have a choice of things you are fundraising for)?
5. Have you tailored your proposal to address the particular interests and priorities of the recipient?
6. Have you done enough to establish your credibility?
7. Have you had any personal contact? And do you plan to use this to progress your application?
8. Have you prepared a realistic budget?
9. Have you been specific? And have you asked for what you need?
10. Have you set a target for the amount you need to raise to get the project started?
11. Is your proposal concise, factual, and to the point?
12. Have you assumed that people know what you are talking about? Check for jargon, initials, and acronyms, and other things that people may not understand.

Source: adapted from Norton, 1996

Explaining the big picture of funding to NGOs

Figure 6.1 gives a comprehensive introduction to the range of funding options that are available to developmental CSOs. Fowler identifies three kinds of funding:

- the gift economy (direct and indirect personal giving);
- official aid;
- the market.

He then identifies channels from the global North to the South, or within the North and within the South.

It is interesting to consider what you think are the largest flows of funds, and what are the smallest. Most would agree that Channel 4 (Northern NGOs funding Southern NGOs) and Channel 5 (multilateral and bilateral funds to Southern NGOs) are likely to be the largest, and Channel 6 (Southern government grants to Southern NGOs) and Channel 8 (Southern personal direct or indirect giving to Southern NGOs) are likely to be the smallest. Consider this from your own country's perspective.

It is equally interesting to think through the disparities between who gives what funds to Northern NGOs, and who gives what funds to Southern NGOs. Is this a question of relative wealth or also of the giving culture among people and businesses?

Figure 6.1 The big picture of funding

The meaning of the different channels

Channel 1: Personal giving (direct and indirect) from people in the North to Northern NGOs.

Channel 2: Bilateral and multilateral aid to Northern NGOs from Northern governments.

Channel 3: Northern corporate support or Northern NGO enterprise and investment to Northern NGOs.

Channel 4: Northern NGO funding to Southern NGOs.

Channel 5: Direct multilateral and bilateral aid to Southern NGOs from Northern governments.

Channel 6: Southern government grants from aid or from tax revenue to Southern NGOs.

Channel 7: Southern corporate support or Southern NGO enterprise and investment support to Southern NGOs.

Channel 8: Southern personal direct or indirect giving to Southern NGOs.

Channel 9: Northern government multilateral or bilateral aid to Southern governments.

Source: adapted from Fowler, 2001

References

Fowler, A. (2001) *Striking a Balance: A Guide to Enhancing the Effectiveness of Non-government Organisations in International Development*, London: Earthscan.
Norton, M. (1996) *The World Wide Fundraisers Handbook: A Guide to Fundraising for Southern NGOs and Voluntary Organisations*, London: International Fundraising Group.

CHAPTER 7

Who does your civil society organization need to relate to?

National and local government

All citizens of a country are, to a greater or lesser extent, under the control of the government of that country – bound by the constitution, the laws, the policies, and, very often, a host of local rules, regulations, and ordinances. Any group of citizens who associate together for any purpose, as well as having to meet their responsibilities as citizens, will have to comply with national or local ordinances that refer to local bodies. In some cases, the hand of government is very light – think of the large number of informal savings clubs that exist, for instance, or religious groups and choirs – but in other instances government control is strong and powerful, with centrally controlled student organizations, women's organizations, farmers' organizations, and trade unions.

When you consider what your civil society organization (CSO) is planning to do, you need to consider what the government's possible reaction to or interest in your activities might be, and whether there is value in making overtures to government for collaboration in your planned initiatives. Why might government want to control your CSO's activities?

Many governments that operate within a democratic structure (even when this structure has not been fully realized) want and need to show the people of their country that they are interested in and committed to improving the lives of their citizens. By increasing the standard of living and by making citizens' lives better than they were previously, they will gain the support of the citizens for the political party that has produced the government, and will likely be elected again, or at least be able to defend themselves against accusations from competing political parties that they have not improved people's lives.

Governments collect the resources for their various endeavours to improve the standard of living from taxes (personal or business), from the income of state-owned enterprises, from the natural resources of the country, and from international aid. They want to be able to control those resources so that they can continue with their plans to develop the country and persuade the citizens of their competence as leaders. There is also the possibility that the leaders of the government are very interested in acquiring wealth for themselves by looting from the state budgets, and they want to be able to continue doing this.

http://dx.doi.org/10.3362/9781780449081.007

When CSOs get involved in development work, and particularly when they are successful at it and achieve results, government has a range of possible responses.

Citizens' loyalty

When CSOs act on their own, with little or no government involvement, and with resources that they have raised themselves, irrespective of government, and when they produce demonstrable results that impress the citizenry, it is easy to see, from the perspective of the government, that such organizations are in fact rivals for the people's loyalty. Even if the CSO has absolutely no intention to seek public office, if the citizens feel that, for example, the primary schools run by the CSO are substantially better than the government primary schools, then it is quite likely that the government will consider that the efforts of the CSO are not encouraging the citizens' loyalty to the government and should not be promoted.

Government embarrassment

If the work of the CSO exposes shortcomings in the ways in which the government is managing development (for example, not dealing with scandals, or not facing up to corruption), then the government is likely to be embarrassed by the work of the CSO. If such exposures result in citizens getting angry with government failings, and holding demonstrations or making public attacks, the government will have still less enthusiasm for the work of the CSO.

Government shortcomings

Many governments are unsuccessful in reaching all parts of the country with the same services: some places are harder to reach, more difficult to get government officials to stay in, or ignored intentionally to punish the population for voting against the government party at the last elections. If a CSO establishes itself in such areas and, by doing so, exposes the government's limitations, then the government may see the CSO as causing trouble for it.

Government suspicions

Governments often think of themselves as having the right to govern the country because they have been elected to do so, and, in the case of senior officials, because they have been trained to do so and have a long history of government service. They are suspicious of organizations that are not political rivals (in the sense that they are not competing for political power) but that are definitely interested in the way in which policies are formed and power is exercised. These are not entities with which they have been familiar. This generalized suspicion is shown in many different ways: CSOs are suspected of covertly supporting opposition political parties, of developing alternative power bases that might oppose the government (among farmers, students, women, and so on), of introducing Western values that they do not approve of and that they think may cause instability, or of attracting donor funding to the work of the CSOs and, by implication, away from the government.

There are therefore many reasons why governments could feel antagonistic to CSOs and seek to use the existing laws and regulations to control and oppress them or introduce new laws to do so. A more philosophical perspective is for governments, proud of their democratic credentials, to ask what the legal basis for a CSO is, often in the form of such questions as 'What mandate do you have?' and 'Who voted for you?'

Possible strategies

Against this context, the CSO has to develop a variety of strategies to encourage government collaboration and support. Some possibilities are:

- Proactively encourage government to see and learn about what your CSO is doing. This means holding consultations with local government, with the relevant sectoral ministries of national government, and with parliamentarians to show them the work of your CSO, and asking them if they have any problems with your work. In a situation of government suspicion in Tajikistan, CSOs set up not only visits by government to see the CSOs' work, but also regular round-table meetings in the provinces so that government could be kept up to date.
- Organize public meetings to bring citizens together with government officials. It is sometimes surprising to find how out of touch government officials are about the concerns and feelings of the citizenry. Unless you are dealing with very autocratic government machinery, this may well lead to compromises and accommodations. In Indonesia, the Ministry of Agriculture, in its bid to make Indonesia self-sufficient in rice, insisted that all farmers plant varieties of rice approved by the International Rice Research Institute (IRRI), and banned other strains. When it was pointed out to them by CSOs working with hill farmers that IRRI strains made sense in lowland irrigated fields, but not in upland rain-fed fields, this, together with arguments about in situ preservation of indigenous breeds, enabled a compromise to be made.
- Organize meetings with government officials and parliamentary commissions or committees to present new information as an input to government thinking and policy making, in some cases backed up by international expertise. In Myanmar, the government was concerned about international criticism of its extractive industries (oil, gas, precious stones, and timber), and, encouraged by a local CSO, it agreed to become a candidate nation in the Extractive Industries Transparency Initiative, an international monitoring organization.

- See if there is some area of expertise or excellence that the CSOs can provide to government at a time when it needs a new perspective, or a new
view (often linked to international conferences). If a CSO can provide
the government with what it needs to deliver for its country's position
paper on a particular subject (home-based care for people living with
AIDS (PLWAs), for example), then the CSO is positioning itself as a help
to government, and this help may well be reciprocated.

Businesses

Businesses want to be seen by the government of the country in which they
are operating as good citizens, and they also want to be aware of any risks that
they might suffer and that would detract from their profits. It is unlikely that
CSOs will have a role in the investment choices of businesses, either inside
their country or from outside the country, but they can have a role in the
interface between businesses and citizens, and in helping businesses decide
how they would like to operationalize their interest in being well regarded by
both the government and the people.

One regular feature of business–CSO interaction involves businesses that
are starting up in new areas, often (in the case of mines and dams) remote
areas. They often appreciate that extracting profits from the area (the main
reason for the business's presence there) needs to be tempered by investing
in the development of the area and the people living there. This appreciation
may come from:

- an ethical commitment to 'give something back to the community';
- a risk-averse strategy to avoid riots and demonstrations by local people
angered by the polarization of wealth;
- a common and frequent industry policy of setting up local foundations;
- pressure from political leaders of the affected community.

Setting up a local foundation with funds from the industry, assessing local
organizations with the competence to implement good developmental ideas,
and managing grant making, scholarships, and training are all topics that CSOs
are familiar with. There is therefore a possibility that an industrial enterprise
could contract a CSO to run its social development foundation linked to the
area in which it works.

If we extrapolate from a localized foundation to a business's desire to set up
a development foundation in the country (either for a particular issue, such
as HIV/AIDS and PLWAs, or as a generalized development foundation for the
whole country), again CSOs are a source of knowledge for businesses on how
to do this. A very interesting example of the further dimensions of this idea
comes from the Philippines. Progressive business people, with advice from
CSOs, decided that a development foundation funded by the business sector
(rather than an individual business) would be more effective, and over 150 of
them have contributed to the creation of a very professional national NGO

called the Philippines Business for Social Progress. This is independent of any one business and operates on professional development principles.

Sometimes, businesses approach CSOs to ask for their advice on the role they should take in developing a public-facing image for their business. This often presents dilemmas to the conscientious CSO because:

- the business may be offensive to the CSO (it could be involved in tobacco or gambling, for instance);
- the business may have a very limited idea of development, characterized by occasional charitable donations;
- the business may be most interested in public relations and advertising for itself than in any long-term developmental impact.

The opportunity presented by such an overture, however, may well lead to negotiations and compromises that make developmental sense.

Sometimes CSOs have an expertise and knowledge that the business wants and it is prepared to contract the CSO to provide such services rather than anyone else in the marketplace. The mission of the CSO may have common cause with the economic problem of the business. One frequent example of this is HIV/AIDS education, testing, and treatment (where possible) for businesses that are losing staff at an unacceptable rate. CSOs with expertise in this from their main mission may well find that the workforce of a factory presents another field of work. Another example relates to export-processing industries that employ large numbers of women. In order to manage the problems that result from looking after the infants and children of the female workforce, a CSO may well be contracted to establish crèches and kindergartens.

Donors

There is no doubt that donors have established themselves as important players at the tables where the high stakes of development funding are negotiated. Some countries are dependent on the contributions that international donors make, and these contributions are in turn dependent on the political, strategic, and economic interests of the donor countries. There was a time when the United Nations (UN) was an alternative source of (neutral and objective) funding and advice, but increasingly the UN has become dependent on the funds of large and rich nations operating bilaterally.

CSOs in the global South used to be supported mostly by international NGOs (INGOs) in the North, and these bodies were in turn supported by the citizens of the North through a variety of fund collection and allocation mechanisms. It is more and more common, however, for such INGOs to now be dependent on the same bilateral funds of rich Northern countries.

In theory, this would not be a problem if the funding could be seen as responsive and fungible. But, all too frequently, the very large funds managed by the bilateral agencies are proactive and so tightly controlled that the bureaucratic administration of the funding competes with the purpose and objective of the funds for the time and skills of the CSO in the South. Bilateral agencies decide what they are going to support, and on what terms, and what reporting is required; Southern CSOs can only respond to their 'calls for proposals' and have to learn the particularities of the hoops they have to jump through to get the funds.

Unfortunately, both the Northern bilateral funders and the Southern CSOs are tied in a knot defined by the projects – project funding, project administration, and project reporting. Very few people will argue that projects (administrative periods agreed for the achievement of defined outcomes) reflect real life. The real lives of PLWAs, or indebted farmers, or abused women, or marginalized, landless people is not defined by an arbitrary three- or five-year period of a project that is an administrative convenience of the fund provider. And yet 'the project' has become the unit of currency for development, and the defining of the project by a log frame has become a requirement of donor-funded development.

This is surprising since project plans, while clearly stating what it is hoped will be achieved in the project period, also refer to high-level outcomes or global outcomes. It is realized that the latter will not be achieved during the period of the project, and not by the activities funded by the project on their own. And yet the continuation of the work into a further time period, which is logically sensible, is rarely part of the agreement, and funding stops at the end of the project period with only lip service paid to sustainability.

It is very likely that CSOs are going to be reliant for a substantial part of their work on bilateral donors because, as has been said, such donors often underpin the funds of the UN agencies and the INGOs. So, how can Southern CSOs best relate to Northern bilateral donors?

- Firstly, and very simply, CSOs should find out what they can about the donor that they may be relying on. Does the donor have a track record of professionalism (keeping to its word, delivering funding according to agreements, not renegotiating existing contracts)? Is the CSO happy with the way in which its work with the donor is presented to others? Is the donor knowledgeable about the country and the problems of the country?
- Secondly, what room is there for discussion and negotiation with the donor? Is the attitude of the donor, however politely expressed, one which says that you must comply with our thinking and our procedures? Or is it one in which the CSO's perspectives and issues are given a fair and reasonable hearing?
- Thirdly, CSOs should try to assess how loyal they think donors may be if the CSO has problems with the government of the country. If the CSO considers that the donor ranks good relations with the government above support to the CSO, it should be apprehensive. It is quite possible that, at some point in the relationship it has with the donor, the CSO will have difficulties with the government, and it needs to feel that it

will be supported by the donor. Another aspect of loyalty is the development of a long-term relationship with the donor that is based on mutual admiration of both parties' support for the important work that needs to be done, and not on an administrative and bureaucratic project-based mentality.

- Lastly, CSOs should be concerned about establishing a relationship with a donor that is flexible and responsive to local conditions. If the donor has very precise and definite rules and regulations for the use of its money, and will not allow discussions, modifications, or variations to this, then relations with the donor are likely to be difficult.

Citizens

At the end of the day, the CSO is attempting to improve the lives of the citizens of the country. This may be through an immediate improvement to their situation, such as helping them get access to drinking water; it may be through a more complicated intervention, for example by encouraging the development of savings groups; it may be through attempts to change national policy, such as making sure that all government buildings have wheelchair-accessible ramps; or it may be through more complex and difficult interventions with government – making sure that citizens get the entitlements they are due, and to the standard intended, for instance.

However – and this is a big 'however' – CSOs are not elected or mandated to do these things directly by citizens. Very few CSOs are asked in a direct way to do something about citizens' entitlements, or the formation of savings groups. It is much more common for CSOs to suggest an idea to a group of citizens and to encourage them to agree with the CSO and to become involved with a programme of the CSO's devising. The best CSOs spend a lot of time listening to the issues that are important to citizens and discussing with them what could be done to overcome these issues or problems. However, it is also likely that the CSO, in one way or another, says to the citizens that they have some funding for a particular issue, and they would like to get the citizens to participate in the programme.

Even when the CSO is clearly focused on listening to citizens – and the CSO is probably trying to listen to the particular group of the poorest and the most marginalized – it is unlikely that the CSO is composed of people who suffer from the same problems as those who it is selecting for its attention. There are CSOs that work on problems of PLWAs, people with disabilities, or abused women and that are made up of and run by PLWAs, people with disabilities, or abused women, but these are rare. It is much more common for CSOs to comprise ethical and committed middle-class people who do not suffer from the same problems as their intended beneficiaries, however well intentioned they are.

And, taking the dynamic one stage further, these well-intentioned middle-class people who represent the CSO are likely to be representing the problems of their intended beneficiaries to a third group of people who are even more removed from the problems of those beneficiaries: that is, the donors – be they foreign governments, foreign INGOs, local businesses, local foundations, or local government.

It is complicated and difficult to make sure that the CSOs, which have the best interests of the poor and marginalized at heart, are actually listening to the reality of the poor and marginalized, and are crafting programmes that reflect their interests, their opinions, and their hopes for the future.

One of the hurdles to be overcome is that of the immediate reaction versus the considered response built on experience and knowledge. A group of citizens who are being cheated of their entitlements may, on the one hand, want to respond with a street demonstration to protest about the situation and persuade the powers that be to change it; another group of citizens faced with the same situation may opt to do nothing because they are used to exploitative governments with very little room for reform. A CSO that has been involved in such situations in other parts of the country may have a more nuanced approach and suggest other tactics, based on its knowledge of what works. But, in the end, the citizens have to agree what they are going to do, and this is possibly what the programme agrees to pay for.

Another telling example is the situation with AIDS orphans – a huge problem in many African countries. Very well-intentioned local philanthropists, hugely sympathetic to the miserable situation of such orphans, may strongly urge the building and staffing of lots of orphanages to look after them, and will fiercely protest their willingness to fundraise for this. More experienced people may well have other thoughts about how best to deal with the problem. They may think that taking children out of a family context into an institutionalized one is not good for them; that it is not applicable to African culture, which accepts large and extended families; and that the running costs of such institutions are prohibitive, even if it is possible to raise the capital costs to build them. The CSO may then decide that setting up a system for fostering children, rather than placing them in orphanages, makes more sense. At the end of the day, the decision lies with those who control the money, even if there seems to be strong enthusiasm for a different course of action.

Whenever CSOs get together for conferences, workshops, conventions, and international assemblies, it is likely that they are going to comprise the public benefit kind of organization. As was explained in Chapter 2, this refers to organizations set up to help other people, and to seek funds from other people in order to do so. There are much smaller numbers of active operational CSOs that are mutual benefit organizations, in which people with the same problem or issue work together, and movements in which people have voluntarily coalesced around a topic important to them.

CSOs formed by people with a mutual interest in a topic, and who realize that their working together is likely to result in some benefits for themselves, are usually clear about what they want to do, although there will be discussions about tactics.

CSOs formed by people who want to help other people with whose problems they sympathize, and who have resources that they can bring to the CSO, have to be very sure that they are listening to the affected citizens and are working with them to design programmes that are supported by their intended beneficiaries.

CSOs formed by people who want to help other people with whose problems they sympathize, but who have to seek resources from some third group to enable them to do this, have to be even more careful that they are not imposing their ideas on the people they have decided to help (and who may never have asked to be helped).

One further danger for CSOs relates to those that are politically active or possibly naive: this is the risk of the CSO's support putting local citizens in the firing line (sometimes literally), whereas the members of the CSO face no danger. A human rights defenders' group, a land reform support group, or even a reforestation group, depending on the local situation, may be very vulnerable to attack or discrimination, and this would not be the case if they had not been encouraged by the availability of funds from a CSO. It is a real and present responsibility for CSOs that they may, by their support, encourage citizens to put their heads above the parapet in a way that they would not have done without such support.

This is not to say that local citizens, after due consideration of the risks, may not decide to be politically active, but this has to be *their* decision, and it should not be influenced by the availability of support from the CSO.

CHAPTER 8
Managing advocacy and social accountability

Individuals with views about the direction in which society should be headed often choose to associate together and join civil society organizations (CSOs) as a means of affirming their views. They like to join with others in a common identity and give their views some substance through an organization specifically created for that purpose. They recognize that by adding their voice to others who hold similar values and beliefs, they will have both a stronger voice and greater impact, and they often choose to work in the field of advocacy.

Individuals (and the NGOs to which they belong) choose to engage in advocacy because they are dissatisfied with certain aspects of the society in which they live. If they find that their values and beliefs are not reflected in society, they will seek to persuade others and bring about appropriate change. This is the basis of advocacy.

Advocacy as another strategy for CSOs

CSOs use a variety of strategies to carry out their mission. Those in common use include:

- service delivery: to improve people's livelihoods and physical well-being;
- empowerment: so that individually and collectively people are able to instigate their own development;
- encouragement of self-help: by building up people's organizations and people's initiatives;
- public information and education: so that people individually and collectively are aware of issues that affect their own development.

In some cases CSOs find that their ability to be effective and have an impact through these chosen ways of working are constrained by the situation they find themselves in, composed of a mix of existing laws, or policies, or attitudes, or practice. They realize that they have to try to address these constraints before they can hope to achieve much more through their existing strategies. In such cases, they want to do two things:

- show that existing laws, policies, attitudes, or practice are hindering rather than helping development;
- lobby for changes in them that will allow the CSO (and others) to carry out more and better development work.

http://dx.doi.org/10.3362/9781780449081.008

We call this process of organized pressure for change in laws, policies, practices, and behaviour that are constraining development 'advocacy'. It is another strategy that NGOs can use to supplement their existing strategies in promoting development in general and in implementing their own purpose and mission in particular.

Laws, policies, practices, and behaviour

Advocacy can operate to bring about change in four different arenas – laws, policies, practices, and behaviour – but we need some examples to be clear what this means. Here are examples from these four different arenas taken from Africa, but relevant globally.

Laws

Laws are duly passed by parliaments and are meant to address contemporary problems and issues, but they are also inherited from the past and may not have been reviewed, re-evaluated, or, if necessary, changed. CSOs sometimes find that the existing laws hinder the work they would like to do.

Take the example of child adoption. Present policies on child adoption are largely based on laws that were passed in the colonial era. These laws refer to a set of circumstances that has long passed, and provide for rules and procedures that are inappropriate for the present, when huge numbers of children who are AIDS orphans need to be considered for adoption or some other kind of organized fostering.

CSOs working with children understand that the AIDS pandemic has produced huge numbers of orphans from parents who have died of AIDS. Society has to deal with this overwhelming problem – and one of the likely means of addressing this is by encouraging more families to foster and adopt AIDS orphans. In many countries, however, the existing laws constrain rather than support such efforts because they are cumbersome, out of date, and ill-suited to present circumstances. The CSOs who want to work with children in need therefore realize that they need to address the problem of changing outdated and inappropriate *laws* to allow them to be more effective.

Policies

Policies are instructions and guidelines within the framework of the law which are issued by ministries or other kinds of government agency. The policies are often the result of some strong lobbying by vested commercial interests that would like to increase their market share. Government departments put their resources behind the policies that they have promulgated.

Let us take the example of the policies of a Ministry of Agriculture. In many countries, this ministry promotes a policy of smallholder or peasant farmer production of food crops based on the heavy application of fertilizers and insecticides, and the use of purchased hybrid seeds. In their opinion, such a policy will lead to greater production of food for citizens' consumption, and food crops will be profitable for the small farmer to sell on the market even though the cost of inputs is substantial.

Many CSOs point out that the availability and cost of the inputs (seeds, fertilizers, and insecticides) are both so unpredictable and so high that small-scale farmers are better advised to have a low-input approach to growing food crops: using organic fertilization (manure and nitrogen-fixing plants), no insecticides, and open pollinated varieties. They suggest that yields may be slightly lower, but that costs will be considerably less. They advocate a change in Ministry of Agriculture *policies* that will concentrate more on realistic possibilities for poor farmers who cannot afford, or who cannot access, expensive inputs. Such a change in policy would bring the significant resources of the Ministry of Agriculture behind what is at present the practice of a minority of farmers.

Practices

Practices are what actually happens, not decided by law, and not a matter of deliberate policy. They are problems that exist, usually in institutions, because there are no laws or policies that cover particular areas of work, or because the laws and policies are ignored, or because no one is paying attention to the human rights of those affected by bad practices.

Let us take the example of the *practices* within jails. The situation of prisoners in many jails is acknowledged to be terrible. Prisoners are kept in filthy, overcrowded conditions; are provided with minimal amounts of food, bedding, and clothing; and are frequently beaten. Moreover, hardened and convicted criminals are kept together with prisoners on remand (and often with underage prisoners, or the children of women prisoners) and considerable physical and sexual abuse between prisoners is not checked.

This is not the result of policy or law: it is existing practice and is allowed to continue. CSOs concerned with human rights feel that prisoners also have rights, and these rights are being abused. They advocate a change in practice through which prisoners are recognized as having certain rights, and these rights are observed by prison authorities.

Behaviour

This is the most complex area for advocacy because behaviour is often condoned by customary or traditional practices, and yet behaviour can be harmful for citizens and can concern CSOs that are interested in improving the quality of life of the people. Behaviour towards women is often such an area.

Let us take the example of sexual *behaviour*. The spread of HIV/AIDS is fuelled by the continuance of certain behavioural practices that increase sexually transmitted diseases. These include polygamy, the acceptance and practice of numerous sexual liaisons (especially by men), the difficulty of wives refusing sex to their husbands even when they suspect that they are infected with HIV/AIDS, the unwillingness of men to use condoms, and men's increasing pursuit of younger girls for sex, sometimes in the belief that sex with a virgin will cure AIDS.

In order to slow the rate of AIDS infection in the population, CSOs are concerned with advocating against these kinds of behaviour, and with advocating for a range of other behaviours linked to safe sex – for example, the right of women to use condoms without risking divorce or being beaten by their husbands. They are working in an arena that is largely unaffected by formal laws, one in which policies are often empty words, and where institutional practices are not relevant.

Later in this chapter we will consider how advocacy can be directed by a CSO in these arenas.

The CSO version of advocacy

In general, the term 'advocacy' means 'organized efforts to effect systematic or incremental change'. It is used for a variety of efforts, together with the word 'lobbying'. It is very common for industries or commercial companies to use lobbying and advocacy to try, for instance, to get an improved tax situation for their products. Such lobbying might well be carried out by professional lobbyists, such as lawyers who push for advantages for their clients.

When we are dealing with value-based organizations such as CSOs, advocacy is not simply about pushing your case in competition with other cases. It includes two specific and particular elements that underline CSOs' specific ways of carrying out development work:

1. the advocacy effort must involve citizens in the advocacy process in order to develop an active civil society;
2. the advocacy effort must benefit specific and identified disadvantaged groups, or must redress situations in which disadvantaged citizens as a whole find themselves.

As well as the particular changes in law, policies, practices, or behaviour under consideration at any one time, NGO advocacy is concerned with principles such as social justice, public participation, a functioning democracy, a reduction in corruption, administrative accountability, and monitoring of established laws and policies.

A definition of 'advocacy' for CSOs concerned with development may be:

A systematic, democratic, and organized effort by CSOs to change, influence, or initiate policies, laws, practices, and behaviour so that disadvantaged citizens in particular, or all citizens in general, will benefit.

Some CSOs do not turn to advocacy because of blockages to the work that they want to do: they are already defined by advocacy work. These are the organizations that have decided their main activity is advocacy to promote different kinds of good governance practices – social justice, integrity, human rights, anti-corruption, and rule of law.

Such CSOs try to hold the government to account for what it has proclaimed publicly either through party political manifestos, or through duly passed laws. They try to ensure that political rhetoric is actually put into practice, that international treaties are actually followed, and that injustices are confronted. They often look on themselves as being 'watchdog' CSOs.

Advocacy takes place within the political arena

For many people, the word 'politics' has acquired only one meaning: party politics. In spite of early euphoria with the freedom to have party politics, many people are now unhappy with party politics and the words have many negative connotations connected with bribery, corruption, repression, control, exploitation, greed, and so on. Since advocacy takes place within the political arena – the arena of decision making, and of managing and planning the use of resources – it is important for advocacy planners to clarify their own perceptions of politics, and to be clear that all politics (with a small 'p') does not have to be the same as party politics. A useful distinction can thus be made between politics spelled with a small 'p', which means decision making negotiated between different interests and interest groups, and Politics with a big 'P', which refers to the conduct of political parties.

Those interested in entering the field of advocacy need to be clear that they will be required to be political (small 'p') but not Political (big 'P'). Politics in the small 'p' sense involves many aspects that are crucial to advocacy, such as reconciling diverse interests, achieving consensus and resolving conflicts, being aware of issues, being able to analyse them and strategize to meet objectives, and being knowledgeable about community needs and concerns. We can think of politicians (with a small 'p') as being activists, organizers, achievers, advocates, analysts, managers, mobilizers, strategists, and leaders. When they understand this, those preparing to undertake advocacy accept that they are acting as politicians (small 'p'), and that this is nothing to be ashamed about.

However, everyone involved in advocacy needs to be distinguished from the party Politician (big 'P'), who is often seen as being untrustworthy, exploitative, unprincipled, and even as a liar, a thief, and a cheat.

A vision of a better world

Most CSOs and community-based organizations (CBOs) within the civil society sector that are interested in acquiring advocacy skills start from a background in development projects – except for those who take on the 'watchdog' role.

They tend to think about meeting basic needs or solving community problems through their activities. Their preoccupation with present problems often confines them to short-term services to alleviate symptoms. Although most CSOs and CBOs have goals of social change, they do not usually articulate a long-term view of that change, of how they would like the world to be, and how they will get there.

In contrast, CSOs that are concerned with advocacy have looked at the present and have seen structural problems that need to be changed. They have a view of a better world in which these problems are eradicated, and in which change has taken place. They have a political vision and a long-term outlook for change.

It is important that all CSOs who want to work with advocacy start to practise thinking about the world they would like to create through the changes for which they are advocating. It is important that they have a view of the future in respect of the particular topic of their advocacy, rather than just concentrating on the problems. The list below illustrates this using the examples from the start of the chapter:

- NGOs concerned with AIDS orphans should be able to imagine a future world in which relevant adoption and fostering laws have been put in place and are operational.
- NGOs concerned with peasant agriculture must be able to visualize a world in which the Ministry of Agriculture supports organic fertilization and open pollinated seeds.
- NGOs involved in prisoners' rights should be able to imagine prisons in which the abuses of the present have been replaced with humane treatment of prisoners.
- NGOs involved with HIV/AIDS must be able to imagine a world in which considerable changes have taken place in individuals' responsible sexual behaviour.

If the NGO staff are unable to visualize such a world, then their advocacy efforts are likely to be insubstantial dreams or unrealistic desires. *Advocacy deals with realistic and pragmatic plans to achieve change in laws, policies, practices, and behaviour, not vague hopes of a better world.*

Relations between CSOs and communities and/or constituencies[1]

Communities

While relations between CSOs and government are important from the point of view of promoting the advocacy issues that CSOs are concerned about, relations between CSOs and communities and/or constituencies are important from the point of view of the legitimacy of the advocacy issues – and the mandate that CSOs have been given from a community or constituency to advocate on their behalf.

By and large, CSOs work with communities – that is, people who are all experiencing the same situation. The word 'community', however, is used in a number of different ways. It may mean (and often does mean) a group of people who all live in a geographic area, such as a village community or an urban slum community. But it can also mean people who, for instance, work together ('the community of plantation workers'), belong to the same association ('the community of Batak people'), or have some other common feature ('the expatriate community', 'the trans-migrant community', 'the refugee community'). People belong to a community passively, being numbered within a group of people who share some feature in common, unless that community is activated for some purpose. If that purpose is advocacy on some issue, the community becomes a constituency.

Constituencies

In advocacy, a constituency consists of two kinds of people:

- people who have a direct stake in finding a solution to a problem that can be addressed by an advocacy effort;
- people who may not be directly affected by a problem, but who care deeply about having it solved.

It is no longer a group of people who have some passive common feature, but a group of people who are united by a direct or indirect desire for change.

When a constituency has been formed for an advocacy issue, then there are some added expectations and responsibilities between the proactive organization moving the advocacy process forward (usually a CSO) and its constituency. The CSO has to be responsive and accountable to its constituency. It has to be able to answer the following questions:

- Has a community become a constituency for a particular advocacy issue?
- How does the CSO know what the communities want?
- How are communities involved in the CSO's process of deciding which advocacy issues are important?
- Who speaks for whom on the advocacy issue and with what authority?

For many CSOs, this new way of looking at a community involves some shifts of attitude. It is not uncommon for CSOs to look at the members of the communities with which they work as passive beneficiaries of services, and people who have to be educated if they are going to take action.

Advocacy that is intended to expand citizen participation must reflect actual grievances felt by a broad group of people. We are not talking about a few CSO leaders persuading a few policy makers. We are not talking about an advocacy campaign that is cooked up in the urban headquarters of the CSO by CSO leaders who assume that they know the nature of the problems faced by poor people in rural or urban communities. We are talking about engaging the people who have a stake in a problem in defining and analysing that problem and determining what changes in law, policy, practice, or behaviour will be a solution to that problem.

It is not uncommon for CSOs to claim that they are acting on behalf of a constituency, but, when pressed, the constituency proves to be very large and diffuse ('the women of Indonesia', for instance). The CSO cannot claim that it has, in any real sense, consulted with the constituency, because the constituency has no real focus. Likewise, the constituency (because it has no real focus) cannot say that it knows the CSO is working on its behalf, or that the CSO has consulted it, or that it has given the CSO any kind of mandate to work on its behalf. A constituency, by definition, knows who they are, and who is representing them.

Risks and benefits for CSOs involved in advocacy[2]

When a CSO decides to move into advocacy work, it is taking up a different strategy with probably a higher profile and greater risks – together with greater potential benefits. It is important that NGOs think about the risks and benefits in advance and assess for themselves their comparative effects on the NGO. Each risk or benefit will have implications for the organization as a whole, since the advocacy work is unlikely to be the only work the organization carries out. The risks could include the following:

- CSOs may lose track of their own mission or may confuse their original mission with a new advocacy mission.
- CSOs may overburden themselves by taking on extra advocacy work.
- CSOs may attract opposition.
- CSOs may be accused of playing 'politics'.
- If the advocacy strategy does not work, CSOs run the risk of becoming demoralized.

But there can also be benefits:

- CSOs may become more popular.
- CSOs may become more effective.
- CSOs may become more respected by government.
- CSOs may become more respected by their constituency.

Above all, advocacy work should be *pragmatic*. It is probably better for a CSO to engage only in advocacy work that it has a chance of winning. The CSO not only has to think about whether the issue is, in theory, winnable; it also has to consider whether it is the best organization to win that issue. Perhaps the CSO should get involved only if it is in coalition with others.

Identifying the target audience to engage

The target audience for your advocacy effort is the person who has the power over the issue or problem that you have identified. You are looking for the key decision maker within the organization that controls the field is which you are interested. The target audience is a person, not an organization, because it is people who make organizations move. The key is firstly to find the organization that has the power or authority to make the necessary changes that you desire, and secondly to find the individual within that organization who has the power to move that organization in the direction you want.

Primary target

Once you have identified the organization and the person that you think is key to making a change with regard to the issue you have identified, consider what their interest is in the issue. Do not assume that he or she is implacably opposed to your position.

CSOs all too frequently assume that all government officials are hostile and all behave in the same way. A CSO that researches the interests of the target audience may find that their position on the advocacy issue is not necessarily what was expected.

In some cases, the target is already convinced of the rightness of the CSO's case, and is looking for an opportunity to make the same changes as those desired by the CSO. In other cases, the target may be sympathetic but is also aware of other pressures that the CSO may not know about. In yet other cases, the target is opposed, but is under pressure from some other quarter that is sympathetic to the CSO's position. A good CSO tries to find out the influences on the target, and the target's interest in the issue.

It may be that the target is not adequately informed about the issue and simply does not understand how important it is. The job of the CSO is then to make sure that it can explain clearly and persuasively the nature and importance of the issue. It should use the language and the type of arguments that will impress the target, and not just assume that stating the issue from the NGO's perspective will convince them.

Secondary target

It may not be that easy for the CSO to get access to the target in order to make its case, or to start negotiating. It may be that the key person is difficult to reach or initially uninterested in talking to the CSO. In such cases, the CSO has to identify a secondary target: the person or persons who can influence the primary target.

Here, the CSO has to think about who is in a position to persuade or have some influence over the target, and this becomes the target that they contact initially. It might be, for instance, that a religious leader has a good deal of influence over the target: in such a case, the CSO targets the religious leader in order to persuade him or her. The plan is then that the secondary target uses his or her influence over the primary target.

Getting access to target audiences

If your CSO has little influence over the target, and your ideas by themselves are not enough to convince them, then you have to think about how your ideas can best be brought to the target's attention with the greatest chance of success. This is where you must think about tactics. Is it possible that someone else (a sympathetic politician, perhaps) can initially take your ideas to the target? Is it possible that you can get access to a conference where you can have your ideas presented, perhaps by someone else? Is it possible that you can arrange for the target to visit a location where the issue is clearly demonstrated and build on that? The smart NGO has to think about all the different tactics that are needed in order to get the issue to the target.

Another important point in your relations with the target is that you should think through the options available to the target if they are convinced of the case that your CSO is making. In some cases, you may find that the target is sympathetic, but they explain that their hands are tied, and that they have no room to move in the direction you would like. The CSO must put itself in the target's shoes, learn as much as possible about their situation, and consider tactics and strategies that would help the target advance the cause the CSO is advocating.

In order to think through these points more practically, let us look at the question of identifying and getting access to primary and secondary targets in relation to the issues suggested earlier in this chapter, when we looked at laws, policies, practices, and behaviour. These ideas are not specific suggestions for advocacy strategies since each CSO would have to study each case on its own merits, but rather they are illustrative examples and possible scenarios.

The law on child adoption

In this case, the CSO is advocating for a change in the law. It is likely that any changes in the law would have to come from a bill introduced by a minister to parliament. The appropriate minister is probably the Minister of Youth, Sports and Child Development. The minister, however, would have to use the services of the Ministry of Legal Affairs to draft a new law. The NGO may not find it easy to get access to the minister, and so it strategizes that getting access to the permanent secretary (the PS) or the planning unit of that ministry is the way to work. It also considers which other people or organizations would be able to influence the minister and identifies them as secondary targets. The NGO may also target the Ministry of Legal Affairs in order to understand more about the legal framework within which a new law might be drafted.

The policy of the Ministry of Agriculture on low-input agriculture

In this case, the CSO is advocating a change in the policy of the Ministry of Agriculture from supporting the use of fertilizer, insecticide, and hybrid seeds to supporting low-input agriculture. The CSO may decide that the target is the PS but secondary targets are the technical advisers in the ministry. The CSO may think that it is important to provide such people with clear evidence of the yields possible with low-input practices so that they have some ammunition to use. Organized groups such as the national farmers' union may need to be convinced first, so that they in turn can lobby the PS. The CSO may think about contacting a member of parliament in an area where fertilizer has been delivered too late, or is inaccessible, and getting him or her to put the case for low-input agriculture to the PS. It may be that a technical adviser from the Food and Agriculture Organization of the United Nations, for instance, is convinced of the rightness of the CSO's case, and can put the arguments in ways that the CSO cannot. It may be that the CSO finds sympathetic contacts inside the Ministry of Agriculture who explain that the real problem is the fertilizer companies who exert a lot of influence in the ministry, and that this needs to be exposed.

Practices within the prisons

In this case, the CSO is advocating for a change in practice among prison staff. The target is probably seen as the director of prisons who has authority over the way in which prisons are run. It may well be that such a person is sympathetic to the CSO's case but feels that they can do little about it because attitudes and practices have become so established, and because the budget of the department is so inadequate. In such a case, the CSO would be best advised to strategize with the director of prisons about how secondary targets could help strengthen the director's case for reform. It might be that a public education campaign about the situation in the prisons could mobilize public opinion for reform. It might be that a foreign donor could be persuaded to assist the government with aid for prison reform. It might be that the CSO can identify people or organizations to train or retrain prison staff in better practices. It may be that high-profile people who have spent some time in prison can be persuasive.

The sexual behaviour of men and women

This is perhaps the most difficult area in which to identify a target since we are dealing with established and cultural patterns of behaviour. The CSO may think that the people who have some ability to effect change in this area are religious and cultural leaders – and so it targets chiefs and bishops or imams (or other religious leaders). It may be that such people are generally sympathetic to the CSO's position but do not view it as seriously as the CSO does. In such cases, the secondary targets could be medical staff, factory owners, or Ministry of Education officials, who can all attest to the seriousness of the situation.

It may be that such people are already convinced of the CSO's position, but are unclear what they can do to exert their influence, and are constrained by social customs about how such topics can be addressed in public. In such cases, it is possible that women's pressure groups can expand the boundaries of the subjects that can be addressed publicly and the CSO can urge cultural and religious leaders to follow their example. The CSO may be able to give the primary targets powerful arguments and helpful presentations that they can use.

The important point in identifying the target audience to engage is that this is not a simple matter. Rather than jumping to conclusions about who should be addressed, and who has the power to effect change, the CSO must think, research, enquire, and probe – where does the power lie, who has the influence, what tools are needed, what pressures are people under, and where are tactical points of entry to the problem?

As we have said before, advocacy is a pragmatic strategy. Advocacy may well be (indeed, must be) fuelled by principles and ethics, indignation and frustration, but it is carried out in the real, political world where people, particularly people who have power, are themselves subject to influences and the power of others.

Now you are ready to plan an advocacy strategy for your CSO, it is time to look systematically at the 10 elements that are necessary for an effective advocacy strategy, and to improve your understanding of the knowledge, skills, and resources required. The very useful list in Box 8.1 comes from CORE, South Africa.

Managing social accountability

In most countries, the government is viewed as the key body providing public services. In some places the services are not, in fact, provided, or are provided piecemeal, or are of low quality – but in most places it is expected that the government will provide services in education, health, and social welfare at a minimum. Services are also available from the private sector, but at a price that is sometimes beyond the reach of poor people. Communities will also provide their own limited services (for example, midwives may be

---

Box 8.1 The 10 elements of an effective advocacy strategy

1. Clearly state the problem or issue that you are addressing.
2. Develop a goal and a set of objectives for the advocacy effort.
3. Identify the target audience(s) to engage.
4. Identify other groups who are affected or could be affected (positively or negatively) through your advocacy campaign.
5. Formulate the advocacy message and identify the media needed to get the message out to the target audience.
6. Prepare a plan of action and schedule of activities.
7. Identify resource requirements (human, organizational, financial).
8. Enlist support from other key players – other NGOs, the public, government, and so on.
9. Identify monitoring and evaluation criteria and indicators.
10. Assess the success or failure of your advocacy effort, and determine your next steps.

Source: reproduced with permission from Camay and Gordon, 1998

available, and community philanthropy for disabled or sick people) and emergency assistance if there are accidents such as fire or high winds. By and large, however, citizens without much money are reliant on the services provided by the government, and the government usually accepts that this is its responsibility. This is part of the social contract between citizens and the government.

Government services can be accessed in different ways: free of cost; by paying the full charge (or fee); by paying a minimum charge (or fee); or by being part of a community that has received a grant from government for some activity, part of which translates into services for selected citizens, such as women or youth.

Government accountability in theory

In general, we expect that government offices near to citizens (local government, for example) will inform those citizens about what services are available and how they can be accessed. We also expect that those providing the services will make it clear what is available on what terms, and will offer some form of complaints mechanism or redress for grievances for citizens to use when services are not delivered, or not delivered to the expectations and standards described.

Government offices that provide services are generally expected to do so in a helpful manner and not cause an increase in citizens' problems. If a government department sets up a clinic to help deal with the health problems of citizens, particularly poor citizens, then the citizens expect that: 1) it will constructively address their health problems; and 2) it will provide the services that it announces, and on the terms that are announced. Citizens need to know what services are offered, at what times, and at what cost. If a government department provides schools to offer education to the children of a community, particularly the children of poor citizens, then those citizens can expect to know what teaching will be provided, by whom, at what frequency, and with what facilities.

Government accountability in reality

The reality is often very different, however. A citizen wanting health services may find the clinic closed, or the staff unavailable, or the medicines unavailable (particularly the free medicines). They may also find that the staff of the clinic are rude or unhelpful, or that they discriminate on the basis of tribe, class, or caste. A parent wanting their child to be educated may find that the teacher is not present, the classes are too big to be useful, and there are no school books and little furniture.

This is not usually a situation where the government has openly abrogated its responsibility and told its citizens that they must look after themselves in respect of health and education. It is usually a situation in which the government accepts responsibility for providing such services but does not actually do so, or provides services at a very low standard.

Not surprisingly, citizens believe that the government has the responsibility to provide services (particularly when they know that there are ministries, staff, and budgets for these purposes), and would like to hold government accountable for the services and their quality. If the government's Ministry of Education provides a school, but does not provide teachers, citizens have a right to ask what is happening and why teachers are not provided. It may be that the government plans are delayed, or that the government is requesting communities to provide teachers themselves. In such a case, the community is aware of the situation. It may be, however, that the teachers have been officially provided but they have never turned up for work, or they are working part time because they do not receive their due salaries and have to earn other income.

Citizens can see the difference between the rhetoric and the reality – between what government says it is doing and what it actually does – and they would like some explanation of this and, if possible, some redress for the situation. This is the start of social accountability.

In some cases, the government is open about its limitations. It may say that it will build a school building and provide trained teachers and textbooks, but it has to rely on the community to build and provide school furniture, provide a house for the teacher, and organize something like a parent–teacher association (PTA) to put these ideas into practice. In other cases, the problems come not from openly discussed government limitations, but from poor management of the government services; for example, no one is supervising the teachers or making sure that they actually teach.

Social accountability is about holding government accountable for services that they have agreed to provide but are not doing so, or are not doing so to the standards that were expected. In most cases, it is the citizens who want to hold the government to account, but it is also possible that one part of the government is concerned about the poor services offered by another part of government. In such cases, there is space for a natural collaboration between the citizens and those parts of government that are taking their responsibilities seriously. For instance, the Ministry of Education may also be concerned, along with the citizens, about the fact that many teachers do not turn up to take their lessons, and would be interested in getting information from citizens about this situation and what can be done about it. The Ministry of Health may have worked hard to make sure that medicines (particularly free medicines) are sent to rural health posts and is disappointed to hear that communities cannot find them. There will be a common interest between the relevant department of the Ministry of Health and the citizens to find out what has happened to the medicines. In the case of roads, the relevant ministry may be very keen to make sure that roads are built to a high standard and will therefore not need frequent maintenance. If the ministry hears from citizens that contractors are building substandard roads, it will have a common interest with citizens to ensure that this is corrected.

While it is possible that the government is interested in hearing from grassroots communities about things that can be improved in the delivery of services, it is also possible that this interest is hypocritical. Poor service delivery is often due to the way in which those services have been designed, or it might depend on well-known aspects of corruption that no one in government is prepared to address. For instance, if the government does not pay teachers' salaries, or pays them very late, or pays them very little, it is not surprising that teachers have to seek alternative employment to live their lives. Holding the government accountable for failing to pay teachers, or failing to pay them enough, strikes at a central and significant government failure that requires an openness and honesty that many governments will find difficult. Or, if teachers do not teach much in the schools, reserving their time to teach paying pupils at home, and this has gone on for a long time and is accepted as the norm, it is a major problem to overcome.

The role of CSOs in social accountability

Where do CSOs come into this? CSOs have the possibility of doing the following:

- They can find out what the government's responsibilities and commitments are, and pass this information on to the people who are affected by this. For instance, the government will have announced which medicines are intended to be free in the rural clinics, but very few people in the villages will ever have read such a document, or even know such a document exists (although they may have heard an announcement on the radio).
- They can help citizens to understand the meaning of the government's responsibilities and commitments. For instance, the CSO could list the free medicines and what they should be used to treat, and find out how often such medicines are supplied, what the opening hours of the clinic are, and the times of staff attendance at the clinics.
- They can help citizens understand where responsibility lies for a particular service, and how such a person or institution can be contacted if there is a problem: for example, the name of the doctor, the name and address of the district medical officer, and the contact details for any other local government officials who may be relevant.
- They can help citizens to present their case to relevant government officials, based on evidence, not just rumour or hearsay. For instance, they can organize local citizens to keep a diary that lists the number of times they have asked for particular medicines and have been told either that they are not available or that they have to pay for them. Also, they can help citizens make their case before the representatives of the Ministry of Health, by telling them who to contact, coaching them in making a presentation, and training them in contacting the media to report what is going on.

- They can learn more about the people and the interests of the ministry involved, so they can understand who is concerned about the issue and wants to do something about it, and who is ignoring it; who is aware of corruption taking place (and perhaps who is part of the corruption), and who is trying to reform the situation.

CSOs will play a difficult role in helping those affected by government policies to understand what those polices are and how they are implemented; in helping those who are negatively affected by the policies to do something about them; and in working with those in the government who want to reform abuses of government policy. Their key position is that they are known and trusted by the CBOs that comprise the citizens who are affected, on the one hand, and they have the education and contacts within the government to understand the government's position, on the other. They are not simply neutral go-betweens, however: they are strongly aligned with the poor and marginalized and want to make sure that their position is strengthened.

Relationships between the providers and receivers of services

It is worth reflecting a little on the CBOs that the CSOs will work with – the citizens' groups that represent associations of the people who are affected by government services, for good or ill. CBOs may be local community groups of public-minded people who are formed around village development committees, or local ward or hamlet organizations, but they may also be organizations formed for entirely different purposes, such as savings groups or water users' associations, farmers' clubs, choirs, Koran reading groups, or PTAs. For whatever reason they come together, they are also citizens who use health facilities and parents whose children use schools, and, as such, they are very interested in shortfalls in the services the government is, or is not, providing. Some of the most energetic groups protesting about corruption in the Egyptian Arab Spring were football fan clubs. They came together to shout for their team, but they were also very aware of corruption and its consequences.

Relationships between service providers and service receivers can vary over time. If service receivers get the service they want without any problems, their faith in the organization providing the service will increase. They may even want to contribute to upgrading the quality of the organization providing the service. In this way, if a positive environment can be created, the goodwill of the people towards the service-providing organization increases and the organization becomes more sustainable. It is important to have an exchange of views between service-providing and service-receiving people and organizations. Service providers should regularly seek feedback on the extent to which they have delivered against the needs and desires of their clients. They should also remain alert as to whether the people receiving their services are satisfied with them or not. We can assume that public bodies are accountable to the people only when those who receive their services feel that this is the case.

There are many complaints that citizens make about government services, but unless the government officials make a point of listening to such complaints, it is entirely possible that their appreciation of the depth of citizens' feelings will be very limited. Once a system of feedback has been established – in a consultative rather than a combative atmosphere – service providers may well have their own ideas about how things can be improved. Box 8.2 illustrates complaints that can inspire social accountability initiatives from both citizens and government.

Examples of social accountability tools

The feelings listed in Box 8.2 can lead to frustration and possibly anger. Social accountability suggests a range of tools that can be used in situations like this

---

Box 8.2 Frequent citizens' complaints about public services in Nepal

- Public services are not of a high quality.
- Citizens should not have to beg for public services and goods.
- The process of providing services is unnecessarily complicated.
- Information related to the delivery of public services is not easily accessible.
- Services do not reach those they are targeted to reach.
- Services are not always relevant to the needs and interests of the target groups.
- It is difficult to receive services promptly.
- Openness and transparency are not maintained in the distribution of resources.
- Citizens are unable to hold service providers accountable.
- Citizens are not properly informed about the times, the fees, the processes, and their responsibilities when receiving services.
- Government employees who work against the wishes of citizens are not penalized.
- Compensation is not given to citizens negatively affected by the unnecessary delays of service providers.
- Even though services are publicly communicated (in, for instance, citizens' charters), they may not be accessible.
- No clear information is provided about the services that citizens are entitled to from government offices.
- The budgets of public bodies are not easily known.
- It is not easy to track public expenditure and find out what has been spent.
- The standards for public service delivery are not well known.
- Citizens do not know how to monitor or complain about public services, or about revenue and expenditure.
- It is not well known how citizens and government can work together as joint stakeholders.
- Citizens do not know about how they can plan in collaboration with local authorities or work with them to make joint budgets.

Source: Khadka and Bhatterai, 2011

to allow for a consultative process, to allow structured ways for governments to inform citizens of their entitlements, and to help citizens express their frustrations and their ideas for reform to government. Here are some examples.

Citizens' charter

This is a board displayed outside a government facility offering services that lists what services are available, how much they cost, who to see, and perhaps the opening and closing hours. A citizens' charter provides a commitment to the services that will be provided by public bodies.

Checklist of entitlements

A CSO collects together all the information from different government departments about the services that are meant to be provided (the 'entitlements' of citizens) and lists this information in a small, easily portable booklet that citizens can carry around with them. It is also useful if the booklet lists the laws or statutes that underpin the entitlements.

Budgets of local bodies

Very many local people do not know the process whereby a budget is planned by a local government body, requested up the chain of government offices to the Ministry of Finance, and then comes back in the form of the allowance that has been made for that village, district, or municipality. They also do not know how that budget is spent once it reaches the locality. A CSO can be very useful in introducing local citizens to the concept of budgeting and helping them get access to information about how the budget is used.

Right to information

Right to information (RTI) is also sometimes known as 'access to information' (ATI). This is a very large subject: governments all over the world have been enthusiastic about keeping government information secret from their citizens, and, in so doing, often covering up all manner of corruption and malfeasance. MKSS, a CSO in India, initially claimed the right to know the details of the muster rolls for government food-for-work programmes, and finally succeeded after a great deal of struggle. The reason for the struggle was that the muster rolls were inflated by many 'ghost' names whose benefits were being siphoned off by government officials. Amazingly, this gave birth to a citizens' movement and a national freedom of information law was passed. Now, every Indian citizen can, as his or her right, demand to see government papers.

Civic education

In places where government has not been active or where, for instance, civil disturbance has led to people becoming unfamiliar with government structures and services, it is very valuable for a CSO to remind people of how government is meant to work. This also teaches about the rights and responsibilities of citizens.

Community scorecard

While lip service is often paid to a two-way exchange of information between service providers and service users, this tool demonstrates this in practice. Service users, on one side, are asked to list their grievances and score them for importance; service providers are asked to do the same thing. Then, under the guidance of a sensitive facilitator, the two sides show their lists to each other and seek their response. It can be an eye-opener for service users when they appreciate the difficulties service providers face (late salaries, supplies that are promised but never arrive, out-of-date material, and so on). Finally, the two sides are asked to form a joint action plan that both sides commit to take back to their supporters and try to get action to improve the situation.

Public hearing

This is nothing more than a structured meeting at which citizens and government officials can talk to each other using the services of a facilitator. Whatever is decided in such meetings is acknowledged publicly and people are kept to their commitments.

Additional tools

Social accountability tools are hugely helped by a judicious use of the media, particularly community radio stations. A meeting of 30 people that has produced a consensus on a locally important topic, can, through community radio, be broadcast to 3,000 people, all of whom are then informed that a breakthrough has occurred. Such a process is likely to prevent backsliding and convenient forgetting of the points agreed.

There are many more valuable and useful social accountability tools, but they depend on a commitment by both sides to consult rather than confront, or, if consultation is not working, to make sure that government officials are aware of the strength of feeling being generated by a particular topic – so that they ignore it at their peril!

References

Camay, P. and Gordon, A. (1998) *Advocacy in Southern Africa: Lessons for the Future*, Johannesburg: CORE Johannesburg.

Khadka, K. and Bhatterai, C. (2011) *Sourcebook for 21 Social Accountability Tools*, Kathmandu: Program for Accountability in Nepal and World Bank.

Notes

1. This section adapts work from CORE Johannesburg's advocacy workshops and Interaction's Women's Advocacy Initiative from 1996.
2. This section adapts work from CORE Johannesburg's advocacy workshops from 1996.

CHAPTER 9

How can you sustain your civil society organization over time?

Once you have established your civil society organization (CSO) and have a body of experience behind you, you will probably want to assess what impact you are having in the field that you have chosen, or the cause that you espouse. This will involve an evaluation of the particular programme or project that you are undertaking.

This is less to do with evaluating the outcomes of a particular programme or project and more to do with assessing your ongoing organization so that you feel sure that:

- it is (or still is) a healthy organization;
- it is sustainable;
- it will be able to handle a variety of projects over time;
- it will be able to develop more of its own programmes and projects, once the particular project (and project funding) under discussion is completed;
- it is effective.

The value of an organizational capacity assessment tool for NGOs and CSOs

This chapter introduces a useful tool with which CSOs, or those working with CSOs, can identify the model of what they consider their CSO should be, and how their CSO measures up against this model. It can be adapted to different kinds of CSO. It is called the organizational capacity assessment tool (OCAT).

This enables a CSO to identify its strengths and weaknesses against the model as an important first step in diagnosing the reasons for these strengths and weaknesses, and in planning for the technical, managerial, or organizational development interventions that are required to improve the organizational capacity of the CSO. It is not, by any means, the only tool for this purpose, but it has proved itself useful in a number of countries in the world, and is offered for local modification. It is based on the idea that there are many common denominators in the organizational components of CSOs, together with some local variations.

http://dx.doi.org/10.3362/9781780449081.009

The conceptual background

From the donor's perspective

It is usual for CSO donors to look at CSOs as vehicles for project implementation. In such cases, the donor is interested in whether the CSO can carry out the project under discussion, and it will try to ascertain the capacities of the CSO in relation to that project.

Many commentators have decried this practice, and have encouraged instead the development of the CSO as an organization that may be able to handle a variety of projects over time, and may be able to develop its own programmes and projects once the specific project (and project funding) under discussion is completed. Moreover, examining the capacity of a CSO to carry out a particular project may not give the donor a rounded understanding of the CSO's competence when it may well have other donors who are asking it to carry out other projects at the same time.

From the CSO's perspective

CSOs are also interested in their own organizational development: their own progress towards organizational competence and sustainability. They want to develop beyond the requirements that a donor has of them for a particular project.

While those interested in the organizational development of CSOs (and the civil society sector) are able to diagnose strengths and weaknesses of a CSO by a participatory research, enquiry, and investigation process, this process is limited by the lack of an agreed model of what an ideal CSO should look like. In many countries, there is not a long history of CSOs (although there is usually a long tradition of community-based organizations) and no established tradition for the roles and responsibilities of CSOs. At the same time, there is often increasing pressure from governments and donors to push CSOs into particular roles. An important part of organizational capacity assessment is to establish the model against which you are assessing capacity.

Both donors and CSOs should therefore have an interest in developing an understanding of the parameters of a complete and healthy CSO. There is great value in a tool that will help them understand the elements of a CSO with well-rounded capacity, and that will help them assess their CSO against this model.[1]

What OCAT is and what it is not

What it is

This tool is designed for intermediary NGOs that take funds from some source in order to implement programmes and deliver services to their target group. It is not designed for CSOs that are membership groups helping their own members.

It is a tool that is designed to be used by an organization with the participation of a facilitator who is experienced in its use. It should be accompanied by objective fact finding in cases where the questions have a factual basis, and by detailed discussions in cases where the questions provoke argument.

There may be differences of opinion – not only because of the people involved in the CSO and their ideas, but also because of the nature of the environment and context in which the CSO is working. For instance, if the CSO is working in an environment in which the position of women is very poor, and in which women are exploited and marginalized, whatever the field of work of the CSO, then the CSO might agree that one key area of its competence should be a positive approach to gender. The CSO should create some statements that illustrate competence in this field and that can be scored.

Or, to take another example, if the CSO finds that all its work is vulnerable to the major natural disasters that are a regular occurrence in Bangladesh (floods and cyclones), then the CSO might agree that having a good disaster response capacity is fundamental to being a 'healthy' CSO in Bangladesh.

The advantage of this tool is that it offers a quantifiable way of recording organizational strengths and weaknesses at a particular point in time, thus offering the organization the possibility of repeating the exercise later on and noting the changes, for better or worse.

What it is not

This is not a 'one size fits all' kind of tool, nor a panacea for all problems. It is based on a model put forward as a basis for discussion, a model whose elements need to be interpreted and corroborated (or modified) in each case with each organization. Experience has shown that deciding what an ideal CSO should look like is a very important learning exercise for the CSO – as important as the subsequent exercise of assessing the organization against the model.

Suggestions for using OCAT

Time, place, and facilitator

The NGO that is interested in the use of this tool should arrange at least a two-day meeting for this purpose. It should engage a facilitator who has some experience in the process of organizational capacity assessment, and who has prepared himself or herself by studying the exercise. The place should be one where there are no interruptions so that participants can concentrate on the job in hand.

Participants

The usual primary stakeholders in an NGO are the board, the staff, the volunteers, and the target group or beneficiaries. Secondary stakeholders are donors and the government. The exercise is most useful for the board, staff, and volunteers because they know the organization well. Certain parts of the exercise are very relevant to the target group and beneficiaries, but other parts are probably beyond their experience. The exercise is best done by all parties in one place together.

Introduction

The facilitator should explain that the meeting is intended to help the organization agree on what they should look like, and then to assess how near or far they are to this model. From the results of this exercise, they will be able to work out for themselves what areas of their organization they need to work on in order to make improvements. However, the exercise does not go straight to the areas that the CSO feels to be problems: it starts with an overview of the NGO's 'health'. The facilitator is like a doctor who looks at vital signs (blood, urine, breathing, heartbeat, and so on) to get an overview of the person's health before diagnosing problems. In this case, however, the facilitator is working with the people in a CSO so that together they can examine the elements of their organizational health. The exercise is not a competition with prizes for the best results; it is an examination of the present situation in order to help plan for improvements.

Components of a healthy organization

The facilitator introduces the basic components of a healthy organization (see Box 9.1) and says that experience has shown that these elements are required by an effective and sustainable organization. Participants may disagree, and will have the chance to disagree in the exercise, but these components are put forward as the basic structure for the exercise. The facilitator says that all issues important to the organization will find a place in this structure, but, if they do not, there will be an opportunity for the participants to modify this structure.

Introduction to the full OCAT with indicators

The facilitator passes out the full OCAT with the list of indicators (see Figure 9.1) and asks people to write down their role in the organization (board member, staff, volunteer, target group or beneficiary) but not their name. The facilitator explains that he or she will read out a statement that is concerned with each component (or sub-component) of the questionnaire.

Before doing this, however, it is useful if the facilitator can encourage discussion on the particular capacity area (sub-component) before requesting the scores, to make sure that the participants understand the statements. He or she can ask what happens in the organization when someone is selected for training, for instance, before discussing human resource development. He or she can ask about the last board meeting before discussing governance.

Box 9.1 Components and sub-components of a healthy organization

1. Governance
Executive committee/board/trustees
Vision/mission
Constituency
Leadership
Legal status

2. Management practices
Organizational structure
Information systems
Administrative procedures
Personnel
Planning
Programme development
Programme reporting

3. Human resources
Human resource development
Staff roles
Work organization
Diversity issues
Supervisory practices
Salaries and benefits

4. Financial resources
Accounting
Budgets

Financial and inventory controls
Financial reporting

5. Mission competence
Sectoral expertise
Constituency ownership
Impact assessment

6. External relations
Constituency relations
Inter-NGO collaboration
Government collaboration
Donor relations
Public relations
Local resources
The media

7. Sustainability
Project/programme benefit sustainability
Organizational sustainability
Financial sustainability
Resource base sustainability
Involvement in NGO forums

Such questions and discussions (called 'critical incidents') will ground people in the reality of their organization and reduce any tendency towards wishful thinking.

Once the critical incident discussion is over, the facilitator will read out the statement and ask the following questions:

- Is the statement clear and understandable? (If not, this needs to be clarified – and maybe restated. Try putting it into the vernacular to make it clearer.)
- Is the statement relevant to this organization? (If some participants think it is not, probe with others to make sure that this is a genuinely irrelevant question, and not just a difficult question that one section of the participants would like to have removed.) If it is agreed that the question is irrelevant, then ask everyone to strike it through on their paper.
- What number best reflects your feelings about this statement in relation to the organization? The scores should be from 1 (needs urgent attention and improvement) to 5 (no need for immediate improvement), as shown in Box 9.2.

At the end of each section or component, the facilitator asks whether this has covered the topic, or whether there are other topics that the participants think require an indicator statement and a score.

1.	GOVERNANCE	
1.1.	**Executive committee/board/trustees**	
1.1.1.	An independent governing body (executive committee/board/ trustees) provides oversight to the NGO	1 2 3 4 5
1.1.2.	The executive committee/board/trustees makes policy for the NGO	1 2 3 4 5
1.1.3.	The executive committee/board/trustees represent the interests of the constituency	1 2 3 4 5
1.1.4.	The board helps the NGO with fundraising, public relations, lobbying	1 2 3 4 5
1.1.5.	The board makes sure that the NGO's activities reflect board policy	1 2 3 4 5
1.2.	**Vision/mission**	
1.2.1.	There is a clear and understandable vision and mission for the NGO	1 2 3 4 5
1.2.2.	The vision and mission are clearly understood by the staff, the executive committee/board/trustees, the constituents, the volunteers, and sympathetic outsiders	1 2 3 4 5
1.2.3.	The activities of the NGO reflect and focus the vision and mission of the NGO	1 2 3 4 5
1.3.	**Constituency**	
1.3.1.	The NGO has a recognized constituency	1 2 3 4 5
1.3.2.	The NGO has regular and participatory links to its constituency	1 2 3 4 5
1.3.3.	The NGO helps the constituency to manage its own affairs	1 2 3 4 5
1.3.4.	The NGO recognizes its constituency as a partner in its work	1 2 3 4 5
1.3.5.	The NGO combines advocacy for its constituents along with its service delivery work	1 2 3 4 5
1.4.	**Leadership**	
1.4.1.	The NGO is clear about the functions of the director and the functions of the executive committee/board/trustees	1 2 3 4 5
1.4.2.	Decisions are clearly communicated to those they affect	1 2 3 4 5
1.4.3.	Leaders take decisions after consultation with those who will be affected	1 2 3 4 5
1.4.4.	Leaders help staff understand their contribution to the NGO's mission/purpose	1 2 3 4 5
1.5.	**Legal status**	
1.5.1.	The NGO is legally established	1 2 3 4 5
1.5.2.	The NGO complies with all the legal requirements of its legal identity and registration	1 2 3 4 5
1.5.3.	The NGO is aware of any concessions and allowances that it has a right to (tax etc.)	1 2 3 4 5

Figure 9.1 The full organizational capacity assessment tool (OCAT) with indicators

2.	MANAGEMENT PRACTICES	
2.1.	**Organizational structure**	
2.1.1.	The NGO has a clear and communicated organizational structure	1 2 3 4 5
2.1.2.	The staff of the NGO have clear job descriptions	1 2 3 4 5
2.1.3.	The job descriptions are used in staff appraisal	1 2 3 4 5
2.2.	**Information systems**	
2.2.1.	The NGO collects baseline information about its constituency before starting work	1 2 3 4 5
2.2.2.	The NGO has a regular system for collecting information on its programme activities	1 2 3 4 5
2.2.3.	The NGO regularly collects information on the impact of its work following the baseline information	1 2 3 4 5
2.2.4.	The information collected guides the programme review and the development of new programmes	1 2 3 4 5
2.2.5.	The information collected is used in advocacy on behalf of the constituency	1 2 3 4 5
2.3.	**Administrative procedures**	
2.3.1.	The NGO's administrative procedures are clearly stated and are communicated to all staff	1 2 3 4 5
2.3.2.	Any changes in administrative procedures are discussed with the NGO's staff	1 2 3 4 5
2.4.	**Personnel**	
2.4.1.	The NGO has written terms and conditions of service for its board, staff, and volunteers, and keeps to them	1 2 3 4 5
2.4.2.	Hiring and firing of staff should be implemented by the director following consultation	1 2 3 4 5
2.5.	**Planning**	
2.5.1.	The NGO's plans are consistent with its mission and strategy	1 2 3 4 5
2.5.2.	Planning has a great deal of input from the staff and constituency, particularly those who will be implementing the plans	1 2 3 4 5
2.5.3.	Planning is carried out based on available resources	1 2 3 4 5
2.5.4.	The NGO's plans are reviewed regularly	1 2 3 4 5
2.6.	**Programme development**	
2.6.1.	The NGO designs and implements a programme based on its own assessment of the need, and of its own competence	1 2 3 4 5

(Continued)

2.6.2.	The development of a programme includes a regular review of the programme	1 2 3 4 5
2.6.3.	The NGO involves its constituency in programme design and implementation	1 2 3 4 5
2.6.4.	The NGO identifies indicators of programme success	1 2 3 4 5
2.7.	**Programme reporting**	
2.7.1.	The NGO reports on its work (in a variety of styles) to its donors, to its constituency, to NGOs involved in the same kind of work, to the local council, to involved government ministries/departments, to MPs	1 2 3 4 5
2.7.2.	When the NGO has a particularly interesting experience, it communicates this to other involved people and organizations	1 2 3 4 5
3.	**HUMAN RESOURCES**	
3.1.	**Human resource development**	
3.1.1.	NGOs have regular staff appraisals	1 2 3 4 5
3.1.2.	Training opportunities are linked to the requirements of staff and their ability to improve the NGO's performance	1 2 3 4 5
3.1.3.	Staff capacity assessments are carried out regularly and guide management in the ways they organize development activities	1 2 3 4 5
3.2.	**Staff roles**	
3.2.1.	Staff have clear job descriptions and responsibilities and these are observed by management	1 2 3 4 5
3.2.2.	The management analyses the work that needs to be done and allocates it according to the skills of the staff	1 2 3 4 5
3.2.3.	The NGO identifies ways of improving staff skills where gaps have been identified	1 2 3 4 5
3.3.	**Work organization**	
3.3.1.	The NGO holds effective, efficient, and productive staff meetings	1 2 3 4 5
3.3.2.	Staff do not simply wait for orders, but plan their own work, and consult with others about it	1 2 3 4 5
3.3.3.	The NGO holds regular inter-staff meetings	1 2 3 4 5
3.4.	**Diversity issues**	
3.4.1.	The NGO's board and staff have members from both sexes	1 2 3 4 5
3.4.2.	The board and staff consult the NGO's constituency, but not all sectors of the constituency are represented in the staff and board	1 2 3 4 5

3.5.	**Supervisory practices**	
3.5.1.	The NGO pays attention to cordial and productive relations between staff	1 2 3 4 5
3.5.2.	Conflict is dealt with quickly, firmly, and fairly	1 2 3 4 5
3.5.3.	Staff members feel free to discuss problems with their fellow workers openly	1 2 3 4 5
3.6.	**Salaries and benefits**	
3.6.1.	The NGO pays salaries and benefits at the rate prevailing in private industry, with increased and improved benefits for the lowest paid	1 2 3 4 5
3.6.2.	The NGO's staff are aware that they are working for the disadvantaged, and do not look to the NGO as a source of wealth	1 2 3 4 5
3.6.3.	The highest salary in the NGO is not more than five times the lowest salary in the NGO (although there is an allowance for responsibility)	1 2 3 4 5
4.	**FINANCIAL RESOURCES**	
4.1.	**Accounting**	
4.1.1.	The NGO keeps good, accurate, timely, and informative accounts	1 2 3 4 5
4.1.2.	The director and the senior staff are able to understand the NGO's accounts	1 2 3 4 5
4.1.3.	Separate projects have separate accounts	1 2 3 4 5
4.1.4.	Financial information is used in future planning	1 2 3 4 5
4.2.	**Budgeting**	
4.2.1.	The NGO prepares annual budgets and uses them as a management tool for monitoring expenditure against budget	1 2 3 4 5
4.2.2.	The budgets are planned/drafted by those responsible for spending them, but the final authority lies with the director and the board	1 2 3 4 5
4.3.	**Financial and inventory controls**	
4.3.1.	The NGO keeps clear records for payables, receivables, stock, and inventory	1 2 3 4 5
4.3.2.	The NGO has an external audit (unless its annual expenditure is quite small)	1 2 3 4 5
4.4.	**Financial reporting**	
4.4.1.	The NGO produces accurate financial accounts annually, not later than three months after the end of the financial year	1 2 3 4 5
4.4.2.	The NGO uses the financial report for future planning	1 2 3 4 5
4.4.3.	The NGO copies its financial report to the board, the donor(s), and the registering authority, and makes it available to the public	1 2 3 4 5

(Continued)

5.	**MISSION COMPETENCE**	
5.1	**Sectoral expertise**	
5.1.1.	The NGO contains people with experience and expertise in the relevant field	1 2 3 4 5
5.1.2.	The NGO is able to adapt itself to the changing needs of its constituents	1 2 3 4 5
5.1.3.	The NGO is prepared to expand where this is indicated	1 2 3 4 5
5.2.	**Constituency ownership**	
5.2.1.	The NGO dialogues with the constituency, but also brings its own experience and expertise to bear	1 2 3 4 5
5.2.2.	The NGO helps its constituency to become self-reliant and to do without the NGO	1 2 3 4 5
5.3.	**Impact assessment**	
5.3.1.	The NGO has a system in place to monitor and evaluate its programme/project achievement	1 2 3 4 5
5.3.2.	The NGO knows how to get baseline data, develop indicators, monitor progress against indicators, and evaluate programmes	1 2 3 4 5
6.	**EXTERNAL RELATIONS**	
6.1.	**Constituency relations**	
6.1.1.	The NGO is accessible to its constituency	1 2 3 4 5
6.1.2.	The NGO listens to its constituency and does not operate in a top-down manner	1 2 3 4 5
6.2.	**Inter-NGO collaboration**	
6.2.1.	The NGO belongs to inter-NGO organizations/networks in its own sector	1 2 3 4 5
6.2.2.	The NGO is ready to consider belonging to coalitions of NGOs in its own area, in the country as a whole, or for a limited objective	1 2 3 4 5
6.2.3.	The NGO is respected by its peer organizations	1 2 3 4 5
6.3.	**Government collaboration**	
6.3.1.	The NGO is seen as a full and credible partner by the government	1 2 3 4 5
6.3.2.	The NGO collaborates with the government in the same sector and in the same geographical area	1 2 3 4 5
6.3.3.	The NGO puts forward advocacy suggestions to the government	1 2 3 4 5
6.4.	**Donor relations**	
6.4.1.	The NGO has a relationship of mutual respect with the donor	1 2 3 4 5

6.5.	**Public relations**	
6.5.1.	The NGO has, and makes available, a public information document on itself	1 2 3 4 5
6.5.2.	The NGO is well known for its activities in its own area	1 2 3 4 5
6.6.	**Local resources**	
6.6.1.	The NGO has good relations with the private business sector	1 2 3 4 5
6.6.2.	The NGO accesses local resources	1 2 3 4 5
6.7.	**Media**	
6.7.1.	The NGO is known to the media and is respected by them	1 2 3 4 5
6.7.2.	The NGO introduces itself to the media	1 2 3 4 5
7.	**SUSTAINABILITY**	
7.1.	**Programme/benefit sustainability**	
7.1.1.	The NGO systematically checks with the constituents that they have received benefits from the NGO	1 2 3 4 5
7.1.2.	The constituency acknowledges that they have benefited from the NGO's programme	1 2 3 4 5
7.1.3.	The NGO works with local organizations and institutions	1 2 3 4 5
7.1.4.	The NGO has plans for its own continuity	1 2 3 4 5
7.2	**Organizational sustainability**	
7.2.1.	The NGO builds partnerships with other organizations	1 2 3 4 5
7.2.2.	The NGO understands what its role and the role of others is in development	1 2 3 4 5
7.2.3.	The NGO is involved in coalitions, networks, and umbrella organizations	1 2 3 4 5
7.2.4.	The NGO has links to specialized institutions that may be useful to it	1 2 3 4 5
7.3.	**Financial sustainability**	
7.3.1.	The NGO is able to explain its need for funds to potential donors	1 2 3 4 5
7.3.2.	The NGO realizes the need for a variety of both foreign and local funding sources	1 2 3 4 5
7.3.3.	The NGO has a varied resource base	1 2 3 4 5
7.4.	**Resource base sustainability**	
7.4.1.	The NGO realizes the importance of financial sustainability	1 2 3 4 5
7.4.2.	The NGO has some savings and reserves to cushion it in times of funding shortfall	1 2 3 4 5
7.4.3.	The NGO has a variety of funding sources	1 2 3 4 5

Box 9.2 Scoring OCAT	
Score	Interpretation
1	This issue in the NGO needs urgent attention and improvement
2	This issue needs attention and could be improved
3	This issue needs to be examined further
4	This issue is basically well handled
5	On this issue there is no need for immediate improvement

At the end of the whole exercise, the facilitator asks the same question: 'Has this exercise covered all the elements of a healthy NGO?' If someone suggests a new indicator, the facilitator asks for discussion, and, if there is general agreement, formulates a new statement, and then asks everyone to write it in the appropriate section and score it. An example might be on the topic of a pro-women policy, for instance. Such an indicator does not appear in the following OCATs, but, in a country where women are oppressed, it might be considered an important extra indicator for a healthy NGO.

Participants can have different responses to the model of a healthy NGO. In many cases, it is possible (or even likely) that participants will be surprised at what is suggested for the ideal NGO (for instance, 'Any changes in administrative procedures are discussed with the NGO's staff', which appears as 2.3.2 in the questionnaire in Figure 9.1). The subject then needs to be debated: what happens when this is not the case? And what happens when it is the case? The debate should continue until there is agreement about whether such a feature is indeed part of a model NGO (it can be taken to a vote if there is no consensus). If it is agreed, it can be scored; if not, it must be struck out.

In some cases, participants will agree that something is important for a large NGO, but not for them. The facilitator should still ask them to score it, emphasizing that this is not a test but a way of building consensus. Anyway, their NGO may well grow bigger in time.

Collecting and displaying totals

The totalling of the scores can be done either by the participants or by the facilitator. After the participants have gone through the whole questionnaire (with whatever extra questions or deletions are agreed), they are asked to add up their scores for each sub-section and divide the total by the number of questions in that sub-section. Scores will thus be somewhere along a spectrum from 0 to 5 for each sub-section (rounded up to one decimal place).

The facilitator will then collect the scores from the participants – either openly or in confidence – and total an average score for that sub-sector, which he or she displays to the participants.

Component	1			2			3			4			5		
Governance															
Management practices															
Human resources															
Financial resources															
Mission competence															
External relations															
Sustainability															

Figure 9.2 Example of the scores for the main components displayed as a bar graph

Mission competence	1			2			3			4			5		
Sectoral expertise															
Constituency ownership															
Impact assessment															

Figure 9.3 Example of the scores for a sub-component displayed as a bar graph

The facilitator then asks the participants to total their scores for each section (seven in all) and get an average for each section. In the same way, each participant's scores will be collected and the facilitator can display the average score that the participants have given for each section. This works best if these scores can be displayed visually – as a bar graph, for instance (see figures 9.2 and 9.3) – for both the main components and the sub-components. It is important to reiterate that these are *their* scores; no one else is making up these scores about them.

The facilitator may also find it useful to disaggregate the scores by each of the four groups of participants (board members, staff, volunteers, and clients or beneficiaries) and display these totals to the whole group and ask for comments.

It is useful if the scoring is done in one day, and the discussion of the results on the next day. This gives the facilitator the evening to do the calculations and develop the bar charts.

The use of a bar chart

A bar chart can help visually display the results of the OCAT so that people can easily see the implications of their scoring. It is easiest to set up on a computer using an Excel program. Depending on the skills of the Excel user, the bars can be put in manually or through a bar-chart creation facility. The bar chart can display either the major categories or the sub-categories (or both).

Major categories. These help participants look at the relative strengths and weaknesses (i.e. the lengths of the bars) in the major seven categories and reflect on which is longest (denoting least need for improvement) and which is shortest (denoting most need for improvement).

Unfortunately, the averages that are calculated to produce the major category bar chart can obscure important differences in the sub-category bars. The averaging process can smooth out any differences.

Sub-categories. It is therefore important to show the sub-category bars in the bar chart as well. These are able to illustrate more precisely the areas with most need of improvement (the shortest bars) and the areas with least need of improvement (the longest bars).

Even the sub-category bars in the bar chart have been averaged (although to a lesser extent than the major categories) and so have a smoothing out effect. It is therefore useful to be able to look back at the individual indicators or statements and see if there are any that are consistently low or high. This can be done by looking at the worksheet for scoring the OCAT. It is not difficult to trace the consistently low-scoring statements or indicators.

Participants discuss the results

At this point the most useful part of the workshop begins. When presenting the bar chart, it is important for the facilitator to give the participants time to work out the implications of the bar chart for themselves – not to inform them of the implications that he or she has noted. Valuable interpretations are likely to be forthcoming from the participants as they take a position. At one extreme, this could be 'This is what I expected', and at the other 'This is a surprise' – and there will be many points in between.

Participants reflect on which sections (or sub-sections) have the lowest scores (i.e. signifying that they are the issues on which the greatest amount of improvement is needed by the organization). They also debate any differences in the results between the different groups of participants. They deliberate why and how this is so, and they think about what can be done to try to improve the organization's competence in that area.

Variations between different subsets of the organization (for example, between board members and staff or between staff and constituents) can also be very vividly demonstrated through the bar chart. The facilitator should pay attention to any places where the scoring is wildly different between individuals or between groups. It may display different perceptions, but it is more likely to display a misunderstanding of the statement.

If, after going through the exercise, the advocacy NGO sees that it has scored low on, for instance, issues to do with personnel, then this gives the organization a signal that it needs to pay attention to this issue, and try to improve its personnel practices. Similarly, if it scores poorly on financial sustainability, the NGO should consider ways in which it can address this issue and seek more sources of funding, which will enable it to be sustainable.

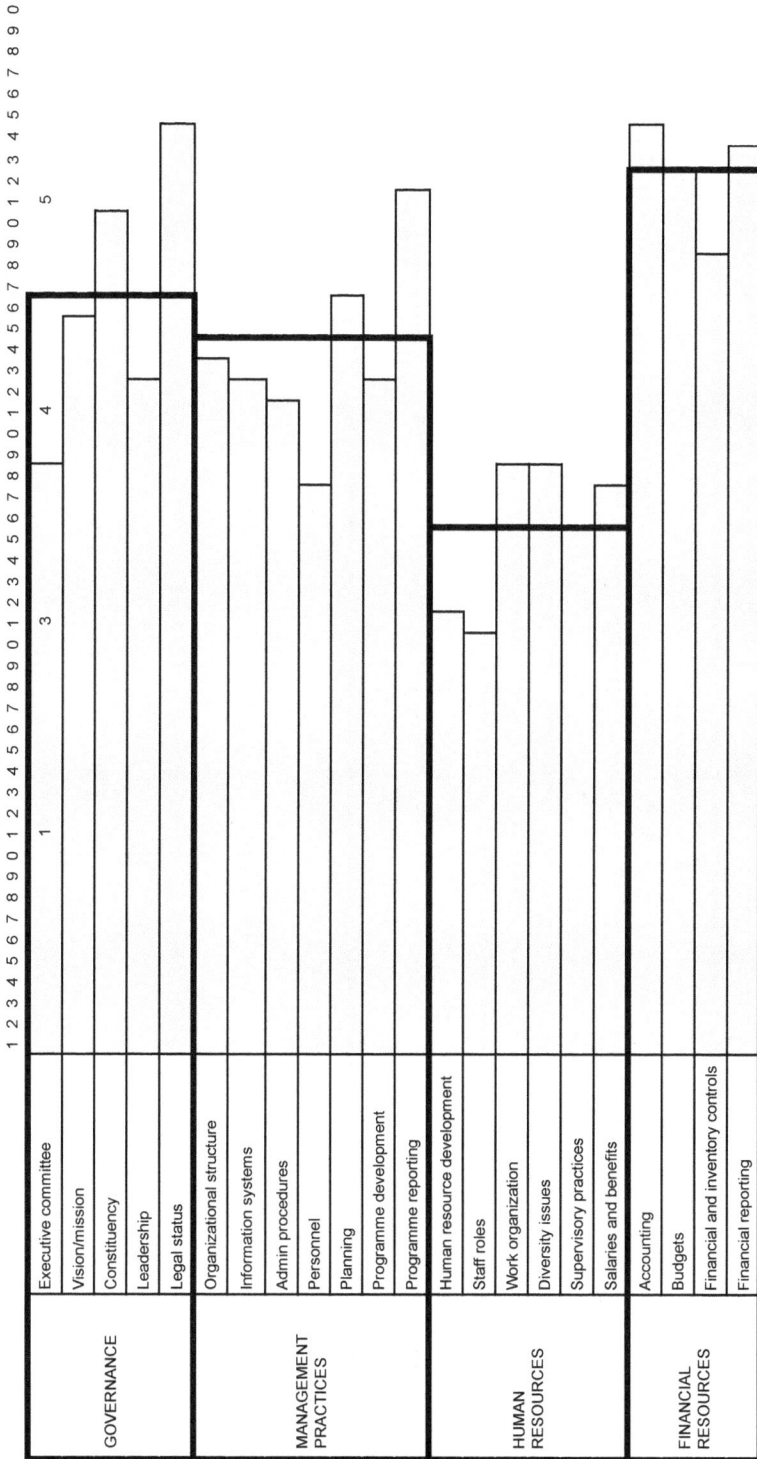

Figure 9.4 OCAT bar chart (*continued*)

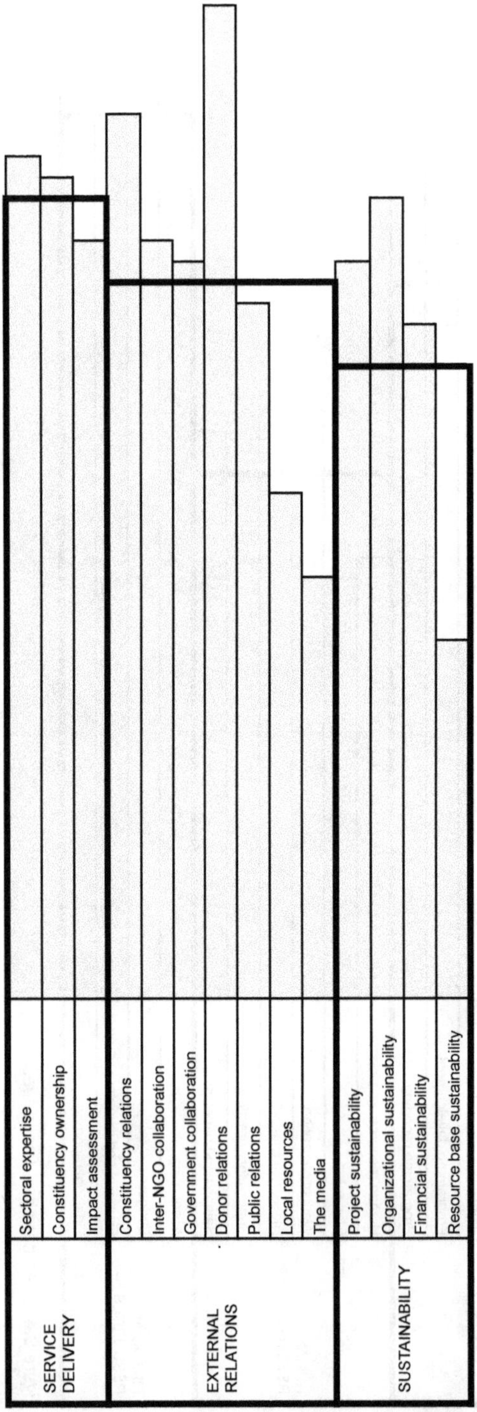

Box 9.3 Stages in an NGO's capacity	
Nascent:	The NGO is at the earliest stages of development. All the components measured are in rudimentary form or non-existent.
Emerging:	The NGO is developing some capacity. Structures for governance, management practices, human resources, financial resources, and service delivery are in place and functioning.
Expanding:	The NGO has a track record of achievement. Its work is recognized by its constituency, the government, the private business sector, and other NGOs active in the same sector.
Mature:	The NGO is fully functioning and sustainable, with a diversified resource base and partnership relationships with national and international networks.

The scores will fit into four categories (or stages) in an NGO's capacity. The facilitator then explains the stages of an NGO's capacity. These stages – nascent, emerging, expanding, and mature – illustrate growth in organizational competence, and can give participants an idea of where their NGO is situated (see Box 9.3).

A very useful reference document from Pact[2] is the *Checklist of Organisational Development: Characteristics of NGOs at Different Stages*. This suggests the characteristics of a CSO at the different stages in its growth (see Figure 9.5). A CSO can look up the area in which they are weak and see what might be expected of an NGO in this area at their level of development.

Cross-checking and ground truthing

Certain information referred to in the statements in the questionnaire is not subjective but relates to demonstrable facts – for instance, information referring to financial accounts, reports, legal registration, and so on. The facilitator should consider the value of checking on these physically (by looking for the audit documents, for example) as a follow-up to the questionnaire exercise, particularly if the organization has given itself a high score but the facilitator knows that there are problems. The facilitator should use his or her acumen to ascertain that the organization has not exaggerated its competences.

Looking for changes over time

If the questionnaire results in recommendations for capacity-building interventions that will help improve the weak areas of the NGO, then it is important to see if these interventions have had any impact. The same exercise can be undertaken after two or three years, for instance, and the scoring compared between the two periods to see whether the participants think that things have improved.

Building capacity

Following the CSO's diagnosis of itself and its health, the organization needs to prescribe a course of treatment that will improve its weak areas. It is, however, useful to look at the whole organization before devoting resources to a particular element of capacity building. It is pointless to concentrate on building capacity in a particular area if the context for that capacity to be used is not there. If a CSO has found itself weak or deficient in a particular part of this checklist, what can it do about it? The answer lies in one or all of the following:

- recognizing the problem and addressing it within the CSO to try to improve the situation;
- recognizing the problem and seeking outside assistance in building skills or competencies to improve the situation, typically by attending a training course;
- recognizing the problem and seeking help from an outside source that will help your specific organization with the problem, typically by getting technical assistance from a consultant;
- generally recognizing the problem, but still being unclear about its details, and seeking help from an organizational development consultant who can assist you to further clarify the problem.

Too many CSOs, when faced with the identification of a problem, respond by sending someone on a training course. This may be an answer, but is not always *the* answer. A newly trained person, for instance, cannot use his or her training if the job description and working structure to which he or she returns does not allow them to do so. This requires a deeper look into how work is organized in the CSO, or it may require a closer look at how staff are managed. It may be that the identified weakness needs some work on organizational foundations before it can be dealt with.

After a year, and following some capacity-building interventions designed to build up its weak areas, the organization can undergo another OCAT and see if there is a perceived difference.

Who can build capacity?

Since CSOs are now a common phenomenon in most countries of the world, organizations and people whose purpose it is to develop CSOs are also relatively common. These may be organizations specifically set up for CSO development, or there may be individuals who work as consultants to the CSO sector. There are also organizations and people who are not specifically connected to the CSO world but who have organizational development skills, usually directed to the commercial world, that may well be useful to NGOs – such as bookkeeping, computer skills, report writing, and so on.

There are also government institutions that train government civil servants in work management, planning, project supervision, and such kinds of skills. These can also be useful to CSOs.

One of the problems is the cost of such services, which are sometimes way beyond what a new NGO can afford. There are two ways to deal with this:

1. In your initial proposal for funding, include costs that relate to organizational development and capacity building. If the donor agrees that these are useful elements of your proposal (and you can make the case that building a new organization requires these more than most), then you will have the money to pay for such interventions.
2. Try to get such services free from volunteers, advisers, and members of your NGO, as their contribution to furthering the goals of the NGO.

Ways of building capacity

All too frequently, CSOs think that the only way in which capacity can be built is through people attending training courses and workshops. However, the particular problems of the CSO are not always dealt with in this format, or are dealt with at too abstract a level. There are many different ways for capacity to be built, as shown in the useful list in Box 9.4.

Reality checks

Even if your advocacy NGO is well structured and managed organizationally, its effectiveness as an organization is dependent on its ability to be relevant to the problems as they are happening. The NGO needs to keep up to date with what is happening, particularly as it relates to the issues with which it is concerned. A very useful exercise that an organization should carry out at least annually is the SWOT analysis (see Chapter 5). SWOT stands for strengths,

---

Box 9.4 The different kinds of capacity building

- Formal training courses away from the workplace (organization specific or shared with other organizations).
- Formal training followed up by consultancy in the workplace.
- Technical, managerial, or organizational assistance in the workplace for a concentrated spell by consultancies.
- Technical, managerial, or organizational assistance in the workplace on a repeated basis ('accompaniment').
- Exposure visits and study tours.
- Secondments.
- Workshops organized in the workplace for staff.
- Workshops organized for organizations with similar problems.
- Home study.

... and combinations of these.

weaknesses, opportunities, and threats, and is a systematic brainstorming process whereby the stakeholders of your NGO consider in turn these different issues for the NGO. They ask the following questions:

- What are our strengths as an organization?
- What are our weaknesses as an organization?
- What opportunities in the external environment now exist for us to be effective? (Update this from the last time you carried out the exercise.)
- What threats are there from the external environment that can hinder our effectiveness? (Again, update this from the last time you carried out the exercise.)

The results of your brainstorming need to be shared widely in the organization as they will give you suggestions about modifications to your activities, possibly to your strategies, and even perhaps to your mission.

Notes

1. All descriptions of the use of OCAT are derived from its use by Pact and use its term 'NGO', not 'CSO'.
2. Pact is a very experienced US international NGO in the field of capacity development.

	Nascent organizations	Emerging organizations	Expanding organizations	Mature organizations
GOVERNANCE				
Executive committee/ board/trustees	• No board or independent body is providing oversight. • The board does not differentiate between oversight and management roles. • If the board is beginning to provide oversight, it may not represent the interests of the constituency. • The board is not assisting management to identify legislators, influence public opinion, or raise funds.	• Members of the board or independent body have been identified but have not yet assumed a leadership role. • The board is attempting to micro-manage rather than provide oversight. • The board is not influencing public opinion or legislators. • The board is not aware of the needs of its constituency or the role it could play.	• The board's membership is stable and functioning. • The board is able to differentiate between its role and that of management. • The board has some members who are leaders in relevant fields but it lacks broader representation. • The board is aware of its responsibility to provide oversight and represent the interests of constituents but is not consistently doing so.	• The board's composition includes leaders in the field of the NGO's mission as well as those capable of carrying out such roles as policy direction, fundraising, public relations, or lobbying. • Mechanisms are in place to obtain appropriate input from constituents and to ensure that organizational planning reflects board policy.
Vision/mission	• The NGO has a vague idea of its mission and the contribution it is attempting to make. • The mission is understood by only one or a few members of the board or senior management. • The activities carried out by members of the NGO may have little relation to the mission.	• The mission may be clarified internally, but it is not widely understood by the public. • The mission is not reflected in planning or job functions.	• The vision and mission are clear to staff, constituents, and outsiders; strategies and objectives are in alignment with the mission. • Operational planning may be conducted by senior management and linked to the budgeting process but with little input from staff or constituents.	• The NGO's vision of the future and specific mission are clear to staff, constituents, and outsiders. • The NGO's strategies are aligned with the mission and state how it will be achieved. • Strategies are realistic in the context of the NGO's activities and can be translated into clear programme objectives.
Constituency	• The NGO's links to its constituency are weak. • The NGO views its constituents as passive beneficiaries rather than as potential partners. • The NGO does not serve as an advocate for its constituency.	• The NGO's outreach to its constituency is improving. • Certain influential members of the constituency may be consulted or invited to participate in some decisions because they are seen to have a stake in the outcome. • Some awareness exists of the possible role of the NGO as an advocate for the constituency.	• The NGO's constituency is well defined and its needs and views are considered in planning and decision making. • The NGO is involved in lobbying and other advocacy functions on behalf of the constituency. • NGO support to build self-help capacities among constituents is still sporadic.	• The NGO's constituency is well defined and regularly involved in the planning process. • The NGO recognizes constituents as partners. • The NGO supports the creation of community structures and develops constituents' capacity in planning and decision making. • The NGO engages in advocacy and lobbying activities on behalf of constituents.

(continued)

Figure 9.5 Characteristics of CSOs at different stages

	Nascent organizations	Emerging organizations	Expanding organizations	Mature organizations
GOVERNANCE				
Leadership	• There is an individual or a few individuals in the NGO who control most functions. • Management style is directive and staff members provide primarily technical input. • Management does not articulate clearly to staff the NGO's purpose or individual staff members' contribution to the purpose.	• Most decisions are made by the board, sometimes with input from one or two staff members. • Staff have little understanding of how management makes decisions. • Leadership is still seen primarily as directive and controlling, rather than providing meaning and enabling self-direction to employees and monitoring their performance.	• The NGO's links to its constituency are weak. • The NGO views its constituency as passive beneficiaries rather than as potential partners. • The NGO does not serve as an advocate for its constituency.	• Senior management's relationship to staff is more consultative and management decisions are delegated. • Staff increasingly understand, but are not systematically involved in, decision making. • Leadership understands that its primary role is to provide overall direction and monitor performance, but it is still concerned with control.
Legal status	• The NGO may or may not be legally registered and may or may not have obtained whatever fiduciary and taxation status is required by local law. • Management has yet to identify sources of legal, financial, and labour management advice.	• The NGO is registered but has not yet integrated financial and legal advice into planning and management decisions. • The NGO is not in compliance with some local reporting and labour requirements.	• Appropriate expert advice is integrated into planning and management systems. • The NGO is generally in compliance with local reporting, tax, and labour requirements.	• Appropriate expert advice is fully integrated into management decisions. • The NGO is in full compliance with local reporting, tax, and labour requirements. • The NGO assists constituency organizations to obtain the same legal status and compliance capacity.
MANAGEMENT PRACTICES				
Organizational structure	• The NGO has no clearly defined organizational structure and lines of authority and responsibility are not clearly defined.	• The NGO has a defined organizational structure but lines of authority remain unclear and authority tends to be exercised by an individual or a few individuals.	• The NGO has a defined organizational structure with clear lines of authority and responsibility. • The administration of the NGO places emphasis on the areas of responsibility but does not confer the necessary authority on individuals to permit them to operate effectively. • The NGO is not effectively incorporating the organizational structure into assigned tasks nor using it to evaluate staff performance.	• The NGO has a defined organizational structure with clear lines of authority and responsibility. • The NGO's organizational structure has been implemented and is incorporated into job descriptions and work assignments. • The NGO's organizational structure is used in supervisory sessions and performance evaluations.

Figure 9.5 Characteristics of CSOs at different stages (*continued*)

Information systems	• No system exists within the NGO to collect, analyse, or disseminate data. • Information is collected randomly and manually.	• A rudimentary electronic management information system (MIS) is in place but it is not accessible to all staff. • Data utilization potential is not understood. • Computers are used primarily for word-processing and bookkeeping.	• An MIS is operational and most staff have access to it. • The MIS is still primarily used for word-processing and bookkeeping but individual staff understand and use data on an ad hoc basis. • There is no mechanism for integrating MIS information into the NGO's planning process.	• The MIS has the capacity to store and process baseline and survey data. • Data analysis capability is relatively sophisticated. • There is improved project planning based on analysis of data provided by the MIS. • MIS data has been integrated into operational planning and decision making.
Administrative procedures	• Administrative procedures are informal and NGO staff lack a common understanding of them.	• Administrative procedures are increasingly formalized. • Filing and recording systems are not being fully utilized. • No administrative manual exists.	• Administrative systems are formalized and functioning. • An administrative manual exists but it is not referred to regularly.	• Administrative procedures are well defined, flexible, and used to clarify situations. • The administrative manual is included in the strategic review process and updated as needed.
Personnel	• There are no formal personnel procedures to administer salaries or benefits or to record personnel data. • Formal employment procedures do not exist.	• Basic personnel administration systems exist but informal employment practices continue. • Positions are not advertised externally and there are no common NGO-wide procedures for determining qualifications for employment, recruitment, hiring, and termination.	• All necessary personnel systems are formalized and implemented. • Occasionally informal mechanisms are used. • The strategic value of human resources and the need to integrate personnel practices into the strategic planning process are not fully understood.	• Personnel systems are understood by all staff. • Staff opinion of human resource policies and procedures is regularly sought. • Formal employment practices are uniformly followed and regularly reviewed to ensure consistency with the mission and policies of the NGO.

(continued)

MANAGEMENT PRACTICES

	Nascent organizations	Emerging organizations	Expanding organizations	Mature organizations
Planning	• Some planning is carried out but with limited input from staff and constituents. • Decisions are made and activities planned without reference to the agreed strategies to achieve the mission. • There is little assessment of the resources required to undertake activities. • One or a few people may make decisions and plan activities, giving little explanation to those responsible for implementation.	• Annual operating plans are developed and reviewed primarily by senior staff without reference to the previous year's planning, analysis of resource availability, or other factors that could affect implementation. • Annual plans are developed with little or no input from constituents or staff.	• Strategic and short-term planning is conducted primarily by senior management. • Staff and constituents may have some input into planning but they are not involved in decision making. • There is an occasional review of work plans.	• There is an annual review of the NGO's achievements and an analysis of resource availability. • All parts of the organization develop annual operating plans aligned with the NGO's mission and strategies. • There is regular review of long-term plans.
Programme development	• Programme development is largely donor- or staff-driven and funded and is managed on a project-by-project basis. • Programme design, implementation, and monitoring and evaluation, if done, are carried out based on the donor's requirements. • Often, the donor's system is not well understood, is poorly implemented, and badly managed.	• Individual projects are developed within an overall programmatic framework. • Occasional evaluations are conducted at the request of donors and undertaken by outsiders. • Constituents are involved only as recipients of a programme. • No comprehensive system exists for determining the purpose and objectives of programmes or projects or for monitoring and evaluation.	• A comprehensive system exists for programme development and implementation. • This system is sometimes one imposed by the donor or one that has been developed by the NGO itself. • Either system can provide the information required by the donor and allows for monitoring and evaluation to be carried out by staff. • Constituents are consulted on programme design and involved in implementation and evaluation.	• Constituents serve as partners in programme design, implementation, and evaluation. • Key indicators have been identified for monitoring and evaluation. • Lessons learned from monitoring and evaluation are applied to future activities.
Programme reporting	• The NGO does not report on the results of activities or evaluations to constituents. • The NGO is not sharing information based on lessons learned from activities and evaluations.	• The NGO provides information on activities and evaluations only when requested or required by a donor. • The NGO shares information on lessons learned only as required.	• The NGO occasionally publishes the results of its activities and evaluations but it does not have a system for distribution. • The NGO does not yet have an effective system through which to share information on lessons learned from its experience.	• The NGO has a system in place to regularly publish and distribute information to donors, constituents, government, and other interested NGOs on the results of its activities and other relevant issues.

Figure 9.5 Characteristics of CSOs at different stages (continued)

HUMAN RESOURCES

Human resource development	• The NGO conducts no systematic assessment of staff performance on which to plan for changes or improvements. • The NGO is unable to plan for change to improve the performance of individuals through better work planning, training, development, or promotion. • There is little or no understanding of the relationship between staff performance and the achievement of the NGO's objectives.	• There is a better match between staff responsibilities and skill requirements. • A staff evaluation system may exist but it is not necessarily based on job performance. • The NGO has identified resources with which to conduct ad hoc training of staff.	• The NGO has a performance-based appraisal system in place. • Staff are assigned and promoted according to their job performance. • Staff development needs are assessed and used to develop training plans.	• A performance-based management system exists to meet the needs of the NGO's human resource development. • Training plans are regularly updated according to the performance improvement and career development needs of the staff, and a human resource development plan exists. • The human resource development plan is integrated with the NGO's strategic plan.
Staff roles	• The NGO has no particular process to determine the relationship between human resource needs and programme objectives. • The roles and job responsibilities of existing staff are unclear and changeable. • The limited staff are expected to carry out responsibilities beyond their expertise and some essential tasks are not done by anyone. • Job descriptions and work responsibilities are not documented. • Job performance is not assessed and there is no planning done to improve the performance of staff through better work planning, training, development, or promotion. • The relationship between staff performance and the achievement of the NGO's programme objectives is not understood.	• Jobs are well defined and documented in job descriptions and work assignments. • There is beginning to be a link between senior staff responsibilities and their expertise but some gaps continue to exist in skill requirements. • Job descriptions do exist, usually based on a supervisor's idea of the work to be accomplished. • A staff evaluation system may exist but it is not necessarily based on job performance as defined in a job description. • The NGO has identified some resources for the ad hoc training of staff.	• Jobs are well defined and documented in job descriptions and work assignments. • All core skills required to perform job functions exist within the NGO. • A performance-based appraisal system is in place and staff are assigned and promoted according to their performance. • Some human resource planning does take place but it is still not integrated with job performance or the strategic planning process. • A training plan exists based on an assessment of staff development needs.	• The NGO conducts, reviews, and updates an organization-wide analysis of work requirements. • This analysis of work is linked to the NGO's planning priorities and serves as the basis for work assignments. • All skill areas required to carry out the NGO's work are covered by staff and the resources exist to contract out for other needed skills. • Staff performance is monitored and decisions about training and promotion are based on ability and needs. • Human resources planning is integrated with the NGO's strategic plan.

(continued)

HUMAN RESOURCES

	Nascent organizations	Emerging organizations	Expanding organizations	Mature organizations
Work organization	• There is little understanding of the necessity to organize work beyond the issuing of directives. • No mechanisms are in place to coordinate the work activities of different staff. • There is little understanding of the need to work as a team or what it means. • Meetings are irregular, dominated by the interests of a few, and do not have a predetermined purpose and agenda, nor do they not reach concrete conclusions. • Staff provide technical input only and are not involved in or informed of decisions. • No formally recognized lines or mechanisms exist for intra-NGO communication.	• Work is organized by supervisors. • Little attention is paid to work flow or to consciously organizing work beyond work plans. • Individual, unit, or project work plans are developed but these plans are not coordinated across functions. • Regular meetings of staff are conducted according to known procedures. • Selected staff are consulted on some decisions. • Intra-NGO communication is conducted on an informal basis. • Awareness is developing on the part of staff and management that communication breakdowns and overlaps can occur.	• A variety of work methods is used. • Staff are recognized as being able to make useful suggestions about how their own work should be organized. • Team work is encouraged and work plans are shared across units and work sites. • Communications are open and inter-hierarchical. • Staff know how to participate in meetings and are aware of how decisions are made. • Mechanisms exist for vertical and horizontal communication and link organizational unit and project structures.	• Staff teams are self-directed and organize their work around a clear understanding of the NGO's mission and strategies. • Staff are skilled in, and appropriately use, a variety of techniques and methods to meet the NGO's programme objectives. • There is a formal mechanism in place for inter-team planning, coordination, and work review. • Staff are able to shape the way in which they participate with management in making decisions about planning and programme implementation. • Constituents are involved with management in making decisions that directly impact them.
Diversity issues	• The staff and board do not represent the diversity of their constituency or the interests of their stakeholders. • Women receive different status than men and their particular needs are not yet addressed.	• No policy exists but among some levels of the NGO there is some awareness of and interest in the value and need for representation of the various members of the constituency.	• Policies exist to diversify the board and staff but their composition does not yet fully reflect that of the constituents.	• The composition of the board and staff fully represents gender and other diversity among constituents.

Figure 9.5 Characteristics of CSOs at different stages (*continued*)

Supervisory practices	• Relationships among staff members are not yet recognized as an important factor that can impact on the achievement of the NGO's programme objectives. • Conflict among staff members or constituents is not dealt with effectively. • There is little or no awareness of the available practices and techniques with which to develop the NGO's organizational capacities.	• There is some awareness of the importance of staff being able to work together and with diverse groups but it is not yet understood that these skills can be taught and such activities managed. • Some supervisors attempt to mediate conflict but techniques and mechanisms for conflict resolution are not understood.	• The NGO has established and documented grievance procedures. • Some supervisors have received training in mediation techniques and interpersonal and group work skills.	• Supervisors recognize organizational development as an important NGO management function. • The NGO has established policies and methods to develop skills, manage relationships, and measure performance. • The NGO understands that clear work assignments and good implementation by self-directed staff usually result in fewer conflicts. • Staff have been trained in conflict recognition and resolution techniques.
Salary and benefits	• The NGO has not developed a mutually understood system of staff salaries and benefits. • Jobs have not been classified internally according to required skills and responsibility. • Staff salaries are not based on work requirements or the level of performance.	• The staff salary and benefit system is based on position and responsibility. • Salaries not necessarily competitive with those in the external market.	• Jobs have been classified and salaries established according to a system established by the NGO and understood by staff. • Salary increases are based on job performance.	• The NGO's salary and benefit system is sufficiently competitive to attract and retain skilled and competent staff.
FINANCIAL RESOURCES				
Accounting	• The NGO's financial procedures are incomplete. • The NGO's accounts are not yet set up for individual projects and operating funds are not separate. • The NGO's financial reports are incomplete, difficult to understand, and not being produced in a timely way.	• Basic financial recording systems are in place. • Account categories exist and project funds are separated but some cross-project funding takes place. • Financial reports are clearer but still incomplete and with errors. • Financial reports are usually produced on time.	• Financial reports are clear and complete, even as the NGO's funding sources become more complex and varied. • Most of the NGO's funds are separated and it generally tries to avoid cross-project financing.	• The NGO has separate project funds and adequate controls exist to avoid funding across projects. • Reporting and data systems are able to provide useful and timely financial information. • Reports are timely and accurate and provide information useful to the financial planning process.

(continued)

	Nascent organizations	Emerging organizations	Expanding organizations	Mature organizations
FINANCIAL RESOURCES				
Budgeting	• Budgets are inadequate or, if they do exist, are produced because required by donors. • Their use as a management tool is not understood, and the reliability of the projections questionable.	• Budgets are developed for project activities, but there is often over- or underspending by more than 20%. • The executive director or accountant are the only staff who know about and understand budget information.	• Total expenditure is usually within 20% of budget, but actual activity often diverges from budget projections. • Department and organizational unit heads are consulted by financial manager(s) about budget planning and expenditures.	• The NGO's budgets are integral to project management and adjusted as required by project implementation developments. • The budgeting process is integrated with an annual operating planning process. • Senior staff are responsible for the preparation, justification, and management of project budgets.
Financial and inventory controls	• The NGO has no clear procedures for handling payables and receivables and stock controls do not exist. • Audits and external financial reviews are not performed.	• The NGO has established financial controls but has not yet implemented procedures. • Independent audits and external financial reviews are performed rarely and only at the request of a donor.	• The NGO has adequate financial and stock control systems. • Independent audits and external financial reviews are performed periodically at the request of donors.	• The NGO has an excellent system for stock and cash controls and for payables and receivables. • Independent audits and external financial reviews are performed regularly and appropriately.
Financial reporting	• The NGO has no system for reporting on its financial status. • If financial reports are produced, they are donor-driven. • Financial reports are not accurate, complete, or timely.	• The NGO has a system in place to produce financial reports but these are still produced in response to donor demand. • Financial reports are not timely or complete enough to be used in long-term planning.	• The NGO occasionally produces accurate and complete financial reports, which it makes available to the board and management. • The NGO uses financial reports, when available, in long-term planning.	• The NGO regularly produces accurate, complete, and timely financial reports, which it makes available to all appropriate levels. • The NGO uses financial reports in developing long-term plans.
MISSION COMPETENCE				
Sectoral expertise	• The NGO has little operational or programme experience. • The NGO has no sectoral expertise or track record. • The NGO has some good ideas about how to meet the needs of targeted constituencies.	• The NGO has growing expertise in its targeted sector. • The NGO has the capacity to access additional expertise as required.	• The NGO is recognized as having significant expertise in its targeted sector and is being invited to contribute to sectoral discussions. • The NGO is able to deliver effective and appropriate services to constituents. • The NGO is beginning to build fee-for-service and other cost recovery mechanisms into its service delivery.	• The NGO is able to adapt programme and other service delivery capacities to reflect the changing needs of its constituency. • The NGO is beginning to extend its service delivery to other constituents. • The NGO is recognized as an expert in its sector by donors, government, and other NGOs.

Figure 9.5 Characteristics of CSOs at different stages (*continued*)

Constituency ownership	• The NGO's services are defined by donors or managers with no involvement from its constituency. • The NGO has no plan to support the development of its constituents' organizational capacity as an objective for sustainability. • The NGO is not providing capacity-building training or technical assistance to its constituents.	• The NGO seeks constituent input into defining services but does not do so in a systematic or comprehensive manner. • The NGO has identified resources for the ad hoc training of constituents in programme or technical areas. • The NGO has not identified resources to support organizational capacity building of its constituents.	• The NGO has mechanisms in place to involve its constituents in project planning and implementation and in monitoring and evaluation. • The NGO has plans to transfer management responsibilities to constituents and to provide training and organizational development support to build their capacity.	• The NGO considers its constituents to be equal partners in defining services to be provided and in the management of projects. • The NGO updates its training and organizational development plans according to the improved performance and capacity-building needs of its constituency.
Impact assessment	• The NGO does not have a system to monitor and evaluate programme or project achievements. • The NGO has no mechanism with which to determine impact with which to establish baseline indicators, establish baseline measures, or assess the impact of its activities.	• The NGO is able to evaluate individual projects to determine if projected activities took place as planned and if specific project objectives were achieved. • The NGO has no baseline data or system to monitor its activities.	• The NGO has not identified indicators or collected baseline data with which to monitor project activities. • The NGO is aware of the need to develop project sustainability and measure impact but has not established a system for this.	• The NGO has identified indicators of success for each project goal and carries out activities to gather baseline data, which are used to measure project impact. • The NGO has a plan to sustain its programme achievements and transfer ownership for activities or services to constituents.

EXTERNAL RELATIONS

Constituency relations	• The NGO's agenda is largely donor- and management-driven with little or no input from its constituents. • The NGO is located in an urban centre and its headquarters are a long distance from where it carries out activities, making it difficult to involve constituents effectively. • The NGO develops systems and programmes in a top-down manner.	• The NGO's work is focused in the field and it is viewed as an ally by constituents. • The NGO has credibility with its target constituency and with donors interested in the same programme areas.	• The NGO operates from a field project site. • The NGO involves constituents in decision making. • The NGO views constituents as being responsible for providing counterpart resources. • The NGO provides resources to enable constituents to develop organizational capacity.	• The NGO is seen as a valuable resource by its constituents. • By being field-based, the NGO is able to effectively integrate constituency input into management and programme decisions. • The NGO regards its constituency as a full partner.

(continued)

	Nascent organizations	Emerging organizations	Expanding organizations	Mature organizations
EXTERNAL RELATIONS				
Inter-NGO collaboration	• The NGO does not have experience in working with other NGOs, either local or international. • The NGO is not known or trusted by the NGO community. • The NGO has no plans to work in collaboration with other NGOs active in the same region or same sector.	• The NGO is increasingly known and trusted by others in the NGO community but as yet has little experience in working collaboratively with others.	• The NGO works with international or other local NGOs. • The NGO participates in and supports NGO networks but as yet does not play a leadership role in any NGO coalitions.	• The NGO plays a leadership role in promoting coalitions and participates in a formal association of NGOs. • The NGO can help mediate NGO–NGO or NGO–government conflicts.
Government collaboration	• The NGO's relationship with government is adversarial. • The NGO does not collaborate with government agencies working in the same sectors or geographical area. • The NGO has little understanding of its role in advocacy or the development of public policy.	• The NGO has identified common interests that it shares with government and relations are friendly. • The NGO collaborates with different government agencies or representatives on issues or activities in specific sectors.	• The NGO's relationship with government is friendly and often informal. • The NGO is sometimes called upon by government to carry out specific projects or to collaborate on sectoral issues.	• The NGO is seen as a full and credible partner by the government. • The NGO has formal mechanisms that it uses to collaborate with government, donors, and other NGOs. • The NGO provides input into policy making on issues related to its area of expertise.
Donor relations	• The NGO sees donors as a source of financing activities and has not yet developed a relationship or made contributions to donor forums or agendas.	• The NGO has received funding from donors but has yet to establish a track record or to acquire sufficient credibility to be invited to participate in donor forums.	• The NGO has a proven track record, has established its credibility, and is invited by donors to contribute to discussions on sectoral issues.	• The NGO is viewed as an authority and leader in its sector of expertise and is considered a spokesperson and resource by donors.
Public relations	• The NGO is not well known outside the range of its activities or constituents. • The NGO has no clear image that it articulates or presents to the public. • The NGO has not prepared a document for dissemination that provides information about its objectives or activities.	• The NGO is known in its own community, but does little to promote its activities with the public or with key governmental decision makers. • The NGO understands that public relations are important but has no ability to carry out PR activities.	• The NGO has limited contact with key decision makers and has limited lines of communication with the public. • The NGO has clear ideas on issues but has yet to develop them into a policy platform.	• The NGO has a clear image and message and a policy platform. • The work of the NGO is well known to the public and policy makers, and it is able to use this reputation to attract support when necessary. • The NGO is able to engage decision makers in dialogue on policy issues and may have identified board and staff members to fulfil this function.

Figure 9.5 Characteristics of CSOs at different stages (*continued*)

Local resources	• The NGO tends to view the private business sector with suspicion and distrust. • The NGO does not work in cooperation with any part of the private sector to draw on resources, technical expertise, or influence. • The NGO's programmes are not based on local resource availability.	• The NGO has begun to identify local volunteer support in addition to that which it receives from its constituency. • The NGO seeks technical assistance from some private sector and government resources. • The NGO purchases goods and services from the private sector.	• The NGO draws support from the local private sector and government agencies but project sustainability still depends on continued support from external donors. • The NGO has recruited individuals from the private business sector to serve on its board or as technical advisers.	• The NGO's projects are supported by local entities that contribute to project results and their sustainability. • The NGO has staff members who are aware of and have contacts within the private business sector and among donors. • Collaboration between the NGO and the private business sector is strong and the NGO is considered a community development partner.
Media	• The NGO has no relationship with the media, nor is its work well known to the media.	• The NGO's activities are not known outside its constituency. • The NGO does not yet know how to access or use media to inform the public about its work.	• The NGO has contacts in the media that it uses when it wishes to inform the public about an important issue.	• The NGO knows how to work collaboratively with the media. • The NGO is well known and its opinions and experience are solicited by the media. • The NGO uses the media as a means to inform the public about its work and/or to mount public education campaigns.

SUSTAINABILITY

Programme or benefit sustainability	• The NGO's constituents do not see or feel that they benefit from services or programmes. • The NGO has no understanding of or plan for continuity. • The NGO is not working with local institutions.	• The NGO's constituency recognizes the benefits from services and programmes but does not yet have the means to continue them without assistance from the NGO. • The NGO has yet to develop relationships with local organizations and is not providing capacity-building assistance to them.	• The NGO's constituency recognizes the benefits of and is involved in decision making for services and programmes but does not yet have the mechanisms to continue them without assistance from the NGO. • The NGO has developed relationships with local organizations and is providing training/technical assistance to build capacity but as yet has no phasing-out strategies.	• The NGO's programme activities are important to and owned by the constituents. • The NGO's programme activities can continue due to behavioural changes in the constituency. • The NGO has developed systems for short- and long-term continuity. • The NGO has developed relations with local organizations and phasing-out strategies.

(continued)

SUSTAINABILITY

	Nascent organizations	Emerging organizations	Expanding organizations	Mature organizations
Organizational sustainability	• The NGO lacks a shared vision and skills to interact with other development partners in civil society. • The NGO has no understanding of its role as a partner in development. • The NGO is not involved in coalitions, networks, or umbrella organizations.	• The NGO has a shared vision but as yet lacks the understanding and skills to interact with other development partners. • The NGO is a member of coalitions and networks but is not yet able to provide leadership.	• The NGO has a clear vision of its role and the skills to participate in development activities. • The NGO participates in NGO networks and coalitions but is not yet playing a leadership role in the NGO community. • The NGO is acknowledged to have expertise in a sector but is not recognized as a leader or consulted by donors or government.	• The NGO has a clear vision and understanding of its role as a development partner in building civil society. • The NGO is a leader in forming coalitions and networks with other local NGOs and participates in activities concerning the NGO sector. • The NGO has developed relationships with universities, research institutions, and international NGOs.
Financial sustainability	• The NGO has limited capacity to access funding and does not recognize the need to diversify its resource base. • The NGO has limited capacity to develop project-funding proposals.	• The NGO has begun to understand the need to develop alternative resources but has no concrete direction or plan. • The NGO has no relations with local government or private business sector organizations. • The NGO is able to develop project-funding proposals but does not have ready access to the donor community.	• The NGO has begun to explore alternative resources by developing relationships with government and the private business sector. • The NGO has secured alternative resources such as in-kind and commodities donations and membership fees. • The NGO has begun to diversify its funding base and to develop cost-recovery mechanisms and programmes.	• The NGO has developed and diversified its resource base to continue longer-term activities. • The NGO has developed fee-for-services and other cost-recovery mechanisms built into service delivery. • The NGO has developed and relies on local support for its ongoing activities.
Resource base sustainability	• The NGO's operating funds come from only one source and are raised for one short-term project at a time. • The NGO has little understanding of the need to eventually become self-supporting and has not yet attempted to identify local resources. • The NGO's funding is insufficient to meet plans or to provide project services.	• The NGO has funding to cover short-term project costs and overheads. • The NGO can prepare a multi-year programme budget but is still dependent on a single donor or limited funds. • The NGO is beginning to become aware of local resource generation possibilities but has not yet identified or mobilized them.	• The NGO has funds for short-term expenses but has also developed a medium-term funding plan and strategies. • The NGO is not dependent on a single donor either for overheads or for programme expenses. • The NGO is able to recover a percentage of core costs through locally generated resources (membership fees, fees for services, regular fundraising, etc.).	• The NGO has adequate funds to meet current programme needs, and basic programme delivery can continue even if there is a shortfall in funding. • The NGO is not dependent on any one donor or source of income for overheads or programme expenses. • The NGO has a longer-term plan and strategies exist for it to become more self-supporting and financially independent.

Figure 9.5 Characteristics of CSOs at different stages (*continued*)

CHAPTER 10
Future dangers

If you have come this far with this book, you will be well aware that the author is an enthusiast for civil society organizations (CSOs), believing that they can do things that neither government nor business can do. Look at the astonishing impact of BRAC, the largest NGO in the South, which has not only had tremendous results in Bangladesh, where it started, but has exported its way of working to a variety of disparate countries in East Africa and Southeast Asia. But look also at the huge numbers of very small rotating savings and credit associations all over Indonesia, which have introduced baby weighing and nutritional advice into their very traditional savings clubs.

While remarkable examples can be found and documented (see Holloway and Beauclerk, 2006), and remarkable world leaders in the non-profit, non-government field recognized and rewarded with formal medals, there are recurrent dangers ahead for CSOs as they pursue the vision of their founders, or the re-energized vision of those who are now leading them. In my opinion, the largest of these are:

- foreign donor dependence;
- irrelevance in wider strategic thinking;
- maintaining organizational strength.

Foreign donor dependence

Apart from faith-based organizations, which still keep alive a strong philanthropic tradition of collecting funds for work that they consider worthwhile, and apart from the increasing number of philanthropic foundations founded by businesses in their own country (such as INFOSYS in India), it has become almost standard practice for CSOs to look for support from foreign funding agencies before thinking of anything else.

When you unfailingly take foreign funding, you very often take foreign direction as well, and you find yourself dependent on such funding to such an extent that it is closer to addiction than dependence, and your CSO has difficulty in thinking for itself, let alone standing on its own feet.

A very important point (often given insufficient attention) is that your CSO will have long-term sustainability only if it has local support among the people and the government of its own country. Many aspects of such local support are contradicted by dependence on foreign funds. The following list of risks is adapted from Holloway (2004):

- Foreign funding does not build local support for your CSO's work, nor does it build local supporters. As long as your CSO is seen as being

http://dx.doi.org/10.3362/9781780449081.010

supported by foreign funds, local people will not feel the need to help you with funds or other kinds of support. They will assume that you have money from overseas, and that you can buy whatever you need. Moving people from that preconception to one where they feel that your worthwhile work is worth their support is very difficult.

- Foreign funding makes you politically vulnerable to accusations that you are doing the work only because you are paid to do so, or because you are obeying the instructions of some foreign power that may have some concealed motives in supporting your CSO to the detriment of your country. Development is a political process and foreign funding provides ammunition to detractors – especially to those in government – that you are being used politically by foreigners. To be supported by foreign funds is considered unpatriotic by some, if not subversive.
- On a more philosophic note, foreign funding throws into sharp contrast the very basic contradiction that development CSOs promote and urge self-reliance among the groups they work with, but do not themselves practise what they preach. If self-reliance is an important aspect of development, then the development CSOs should pay as much attention to it as do the people with whom they work.

Irrelevance in wider strategic thinking

It is common among big multilateral development agencies to use 'NGO' or 'CSO' as a dismissive put-down (as in 'That's a very CSO way of looking at the issue'). The basis for this is that the big guns of the development business (large bilaterals such as the UK's Department for International Development and large multilaterals including UNICEF, UNDP, and the World Bank), which command large amounts of money, and with this money large amounts of expertise, feel that they have the insight and the analysis to deal with the really important strategic issues, whereas CSOs have a tendency to work on the periphery, and finally to be unimportant in the wider context of international development.

There is enough truth in this to warrant paying attention to it. Yet, in many, many cases of important development initiatives, it is CSOs that have been the pioneers, and bilateral and multilateral development agencies that have picked up their ideas and run with them. It was a CSO, Transparency International, that identified the huge importance of fighting corruption – and the big development agencies played catch-up. It was a CSO, Médecins Sans Frontières, which had the greatest insight into the recent Ebola epidemic in West Africa, as well as the best operational response to it. It was a CSO, PDA, that drastically reduced the numbers of people with HIV in Thailand.

However, CSOs, as I hope I have shown in Chapter 5 on planning, have a tendency to mistake the symptoms of a social problem for the causes of it, and not to pursue the root causes with enough vigour. I have heard many CSOs say, in response to such an accusation, that they cannot pursue such a path 'because it is too political', meaning that the root causes of a problem are mired in national politics, which is a field where local CSOs are ineffective. All development is political, however, providing we use the small 'p'. It is about the uses and abuses of power, while not necessarily involving party politics. CSOs have got to find a way to get involved in the causes and real issues that keep poor and marginalized people in the states they are in.

There are two linked fields that are opening up in which CSOs can certainly get involved and make a substantial difference.

The first is the field of anti-corruption. Whatever field the CSO is working in – from HIV/AIDS to clean water supplies, from election monitoring to trafficking – experience has taught development organizations that corruption is bound to be an actor. Transparency International, with its large number of national chapters, and all the other CSOs that its example has spawned, has identified ways of getting involved in essential problems and issues that have far-reaching consequences. The resources of the Goldenberg scandal in Kenya, if they had not been stolen but had been put to different uses, could have provided antiretrovirals for all Kenyans with HIV/AIDS.

Nearly every field in which CSOs work has a corruption angle to it, whereby, if the CSOs were able to address it, substantial quantities of national resources (not foreign resources) would be available for development. *Stealing from the People* (Holloway, 2002) identified the amounts of corruption involved in each application for a driving licence in Indonesia, then multiplied this by the number of offices where it took place and the number of working days, and found a colossal amount of funds stolen from the people – and reflected that it was likely a proportion of these funds were passed up the government hierarchy to benefit senior officials and possibly politicians.

The second is the field of social accountability (see Chapter 8), which gives CSOs the opportunity to ask government not about what it has not yet done, but about what it has not done out of the things it promised to do in its laws, policies, edicts, and budgets. This new field, accepted and supported by increasing numbers of big development agencies, allows CSOs to get involved in what would have previously been considered 'too political'. CSOs must take this opportunity and expand their range of work.

Part of this involves the 'building of integrity', in counterpoint to 'combating corruption'. Some of those involved in the start-up of Transparency International split off 10 years ago and formed TIRI, which then became Integrity Action. Its purpose is to build integrity rather than simply to attack corruption. This gives CSOs every opportunity to get involved in essential and very relevant issues, because integrity failures underpin so many development problems.

Maintaining organizational strength

Organizations are the most important unit of development, rather than projects, as is often suggested and often the case in practice. An organization with a long-term vision, on which it keeps its focus, is fundamental to effectiveness: projects come and go depending on the baroque interplay between donors, contractors, and a variety of intermediaries, but if an organization can remain true to itself, it has the opportunity to really make a difference. Think of BRAC, Grameen Bank, PDA, and many others – they were strong enough to keep their focus.

Against this, however, there are many intermediaries that receive funds for 'capacity building' of CSOs, and this translates into delivering mantras – some of which we have used in Chapter 5 (vision, mission, indicators, monitoring, evaluation) – together with large quantities of organizational governance and financial management advice.

It is certainly important for CSOs to be well managed (and the use of the organizational capacity assessment tool will help them work out their own priorities for good management, and then assess how well they are doing), but it is essential that they have a clear idea of: 1) what needs to be done; and 2) what part they will be able to play in what needs to be done. There is a clear danger that too much 'capacity building' will produce CSOs that are managerially impeccable, but not very effective in reducing levels of poverty and marginalization, which was their original purpose.

References

Holloway, R. (ed.) (2002) *Stealing from the People*, 4 volumes, Jakarta: Aksara Foundation and Partnership for Governance Reform in Indonesia.

Holloway, R. (2004) *Towards Financial Self-reliance: A Handbook on Resource Mobilisation for CSOs in the South*, London: Earthscan.

Holloway, R. and Beauclerk, J. (2006) *Beyond NGOs: Civil Society Organisations with Development Impact*, Geneva: Aga Khan Development Network and INTRAC. <http://www.integrityaction.org>.

www.ingramcontent.com/pod-product-compliance
Lightning Source LLC
Chambersburg PA
CBHW060044030426
42334CB00019B/2482